The Burning Breath Chapters

Previous Titles

A View Inside a Medium Secure Unit (*Asylum* magazine, 2019)
The Art of Occupation: Wielding the Mind (*OTNews*, 2019)
The Do of Korean Fighting (*Asylum* magazine, 2019)
Black History and the Struggle to Free Our Minds (*Asylum* magazine, 2020)
The Trauma of Institutionalisation (*Asylum* magazine, 2021)
Health and Highflyers (*OTNews*, 2022)
Escooters: A Social Phenomenon (University of Dundee, 2023)
The Violence Conundrum (*Asylum* magazine, 2024)

What People Are Saying About

The Burning Breath Chapters

Wow, what a read! I felt my heart trembling while reading this powerful, insightful, and compassionate work. With high levels of emotional intelligence and kindness, the authors are truly inspirational, and I have deep respect for their authenticity and passion to support others to transform their lives through mindfulness and self-compassion.
Karen Atkinson, CEO of Mindfulness UK and former chair of the British Mindfulness Society

The Burning Breath Chapters is a powerful and brave collection that speaks directly to the heart of restorative justice. Through poetry, reflection, and lived experiences, the authors create an important space for sharing truths, healing, and transformation. Their voices — shaped by trauma, institutionalisation, and personal growth — invite us to look beyond labels and systems to see the humanity behind the harm. What makes this collection so impactful is its genuine authenticity. It doesn't just talk about change; it embodies it. Writing becomes a way to take responsibility, sharing stories serves as a form of healing, and the creative process empowers individuals. These are the core principles of restorative practice: voice, agency, and community. This book is a valuable resource for anyone involved in justice, mental health, youth work, or education. It serves as a reminder that real change often starts within relationships — in the willingness to listen, understand, and stand beside others on their healing journeys.
James Simon, CEO of Restorative Justice Council

I found *The Burning Breath Chapters* meaningful and encouraging to think about the experiences of other people.
Prue Norton, Head of the MSN Fund

The authors write with insight and significance about factors associated with "the system". This text demonstrates an intrinsic desire to see things change, be more culturally appropriate and empathic with the realities of how an individual might find oneself involved in services. This is profoundly relevant to today's society and should be recommended reading for anyone with an interest in understanding recovery and resilience from a first-hand account.
Nick Hunter, former mental health service user and expert by experience

This is a remarkable book that not only shares the authors' experiences in an accessible and inspirational manner, telling their stories and chronicling their growth, learning, and reflections through prose and poetry; it also shares insights for those of us who work in mental health services with an ambition to drive improvement. These narratives speak from the heart, and Sewell's unique journey is one that allows those of us on the outside to step inside the feelings of mental illness, pain, and disruptive life events. The use of poetry, in particular, is compelling in expressing the feelings behind the actions. Sewell [et al.] marries together the storytelling, poetry, reflection, and learning to build a unique, creative book that drives improvement and change within mental health services and mental health professionals, and I am grateful for that.
Victoria Hart, Head of Social Work and Safeguarding Lead – Forensic Services, South London and Maudsley NHS Foundation Trust

The Burning Breath Chapters

Jerome Sewell, Mase Okor and Jason Harris

London, UK
Washington, DC, USA

First published by Mantra Books, 2026
Mantra Books is an imprint of Collective Ink Ltd.,
Unit 11, Shepperton House, 89 Shepperton Road, London, N1 3DF
office@collectiveinkbooks.com
www.collectiveinkbooks.com
www.mantra-books.net

For distributor details and how to order please visit the 'Ordering' section on our website.

ISBN: 978 1 78535 994 1
978 1 917704 07 6 (ebook)
Library of Congress Control Number: 2025936518

A CIP catalogue record for this book is available from the British Library.

Design: Lapiz Digital Services

UK: Printed and bound by CPI Group (UK) Ltd, Croydon, CR0 4YY
Printed in North America by CPI GPS partners

The manufacturer's authorised representative in the EU for product safety is:
eucomply OÜ - Pärnu mnt 139b-14, 11317 Tallinn, Estonia,
hello@eucompliancepartner.com, www.eucompliancepartner.com

Contents

Preface ix
Acknowledgments xvii

Adolescence in the Hood 1
Where Were You? by Jerome Sewell 5
Isolation by Jason Harris 8
AL(LIEN) ONE by Mase Okor 9
Relationship Building for Service User Support 10
The Struggle of Early Years 12
Burning Breath by Jerome Sewell 16
Practice in the Home Environment 19
Reckless Days of a Teenage Wildness 23
Drunken Pain by Jerome Sewell 27
Drug and Alcohol Interventions During Practice 29
Crime Sagas 32
The Beast and the Garden by Jerome Sewell 36
Changing Service User Perspectives During Practice 40
Falling into Psychosis 43
Reality by Jerome Sewell 47
ALTERNATE ILLUSIONS (A.I.) by Mase Okor 51
Perspectives of Recovery in Practice 51
Journey to the Underworld 55
Through Hell's Gates by Jerome Sewell 58
One of Those Nights by service users from the Bethlem Royal Hospital 61
Into the Frying Pan of a Psychiatric Hospital 63
The Trauma of Institutionalisation by Jerome Sewell 65
The Trauma of Institutionalisation by Jason Harris 66

TRAPPED IN THE REFRAIN by Mase Okor 67
Non-Violence and Rehabilitation 69
Love Yourself by Jerome Sewell 72
Encouraging Self-Compassion in Practice 77
Paths to Freedom 79
Liberty Wind by Jerome Sewell 82
Breathe by Jason Harris 84
Breathe by Mase Okor 85
Redefining Reality in Practice 85
What the Future Held 89
Dreams Dog by Jerome Sewell 95
Lasting Rehabilitation in Practice 98

About the Authors 104
Further Reading 107
References 108

As authors we would like to dedicate this book to God, who has been a consistent source of strength and wisdom across our lives, to our families who have been there for us, and to the many good souls who have assisted our progress in life. We would also like to dedicate this to the many lives we have encountered and been able to add to across our journeys.

Preface

Embarking on the writing of a manuscript can be done for many reasons: money, fame, expression, and purpose. As an artist, from my own point of view my work has over the years been centered on lived experiences and bringing new narratives to the world that explore uncharted dimensions of what are now popular genres. There are some who say a life vocation comes down to a calling — a person has to fulfill something in life — and for myself my calling has seen me partake in what I regard as the sacred task of using various mediums to teach and espouse moral values. *The Burning Breath Chapters* is a piece following in a long line of successive works founded upon this premise. But amidst its writing, it has gotten to a point where I see it as perhaps the most important work so far for myself. In many stories, great sword craftsmen in Japan may create a weapon which represents the highest achievement in their practice; a samurai's heart is said to be in his sword. This manuscript represents this inasmuch as, on my path, life has taught me that it is our values and moral development that comprise the highest occupation of life. As the Zen Buddhist whose writings were fundamental to my rehabilitation said:

> however combative Zen people may seem because of their shouting and stick wielding, just show them a mound of corpses or a river of flowing blood and not one of them will celebrate war. This is precisely the way I feel. The development, advancement, and perfection of our inner capabilities, which may be regarded as the most essential task of our lives, can be effectively accomplished only during times of peace. When peace is lost and people start shooting and slashing at their neighbours, the world becomes the realm of the azures and the demon

> king prevails ... war instantly turns heaven into hell and transforms bodhi into delusion. How could a Zen man assent to it?
> (Professor Kemmyo Taira Sato, *Middle Way*)

Along my career journey I have performed many functions in organizations, working in the criminal justice, youth work, and mental health sectors over the last six years. At a conference I was asked to present at (for social workers across London in 2024), before I was called onto the stage I was introduced as a project manager, executive producer, head of two companies, and a host of other titles, but standing in front of the faces in front of me I clarified that those titles are all well and good but that is not how the journey began. The most recent side of my journey was being convicted in 2015 for a violent crime, sentenced to five years in prison, and then, after 18 months spent there, being sent to a psychiatric hospital. And so, in my context it is my development as a person that defines my life, as well as my service to others, as opposed to accolades and achievements. *The Burning Breath Chapters* represents the culmination of that inward growth; it brings together six years of me working with 400 people in various roles who have faced the sharp end of experiences in life, and this is brought together with insight into the workings of the mind, emotions, and paths of rehabilitation as experienced and learned through mindfulness as a therapeutic intervention (which I have practiced for a longer time still).

Among the 20 interventions and projects I have led to date, my signature as defined among my business partners and funders has been the creation of stories that educate society whilst using the process of artistic creation itself to empower and act as an intervention for those who are dispossessed. To clarify what this means in practice, the creation of my feature film *100 Mistakes* is a good example. This project was based on the creation of a film centered on a screenplay that I wrote about a young man who turns from a life of crime and starts his own business. During the making of the film we hired young offenders as cast and crew members, and they were taught practical skills by production companies, took part in soft skills workshops, and were put forward for industry jobs. When the film was completed it entered distribution and was showcased to local youths in community center presentations. This is a practical example of how I tend to use artistic processes for multifaceted social benefit.

In the same way, *The Burning Breath Chapters* followed a similar path. When the funder, Synergi, first spoke to me about their creative exhibition, I wondered what I could put forward as an artist to a competition based on their theme "Remembrance as Resistance" where they sought to archive and compile the experiences of communities that had been through traumatic events. I decided to submit a poem titled "Burning Breath" which was centered on the healing effect that mindfulness meditation had over my life and traumatic experiences. But after this submission it bothered me; one poem was not enough; it did not say everything I needed to say. And so, the *Burning Breath Chapters* project began, and in line with my signature process I decided that I would bring in the voices and abilities of other poets who share my experiences, onboarding Mase Okor and Jason Harris. It culminated at a perfect point in the history of my company Therapeutic Productions CIC, where we decided we would focus on building partnerships with those who share our experiences; engaging in a higher level of co-production in our work.

Recognizing that mindfulness meditation and Zen philosophy have held a pivotal role in my reformation, turning me from within to become a compassionate person beyond the anger and violence that had held on to me since childhood, and even more than this, keeping me stable although suffering from a severe mental illness, I knew that the three of us had something we needed to add to the discourse: wisdom based on experience and knowledge that would reveal new insight into mindful practice itself. Returning to the analogy of the samurai's sword, *The Burning Breath Chapters* holds the truest account of my knowledge of criminal rehabilitation and mental health recovery to date, infused not just with therapy-based knowledge but the lessons learnt from many lives I have worked with. It truly is a culmination of all sides of me, both professionally and personally. This medium of writing brings all three of us together as writers, and our experiences together form our message. We write for a deeper purpose: the power of ink to heal and define.

Each writer of this manuscript has his own encounter with the power of this medium, as Jason Harris explains:

> At the start of my experience, I began hearing voices externally of a threatening nature. Which put me in a state of confusion, seeking answers but unable to make sense of it all. What was odd was I couldn't see them, but I could hear them as clear as a conversation in a quiet coffee shop. It bothered me so much that I was constantly looking for clues to understand why this was happening. I tried explaining to friends and family, but they too were unsure as they were unable to hear what I was hearing. As a result I became wary of everyone around me; thinking that they were all conspiring against me, including my family. A friend suggested that I should go on holiday for a break but instead I started moving around the UK and abroad looking for somewhere to settle. I eventually ended up in Norfolk where I was arrested and remanded in prison after an altercation. I was later diagnosed with schizophrenia and transferred to a mental health hospital.
>
> One of the many reasons I shared my poetry was to try and help people get a better picture and hopefully some

understanding of how challenging these situations can be for many individuals.

Although I had family and friends around me, I felt very alone with my experience and misunderstood. I think that was because the people that I had around me couldn't feel or relate to what I was experiencing. I also felt ashamed because of the nature of what I was experiencing as well as the stigma that's often attached to the diagnosis. I was worried about how I might be received by others; it often felt like I was withholding a dirty secret. It seems to bring a sense of hopelessness for a number of reasons: being told that you may have this condition for life, along with the weight gain which only made what I was experiencing worse. I have always been an active person, so this was a big issue for me. It led to me isolating myself and feeling unsure about my identity and purpose.

I now know that there are so many people in similar situations who feel alone and isolated. Which is mainly the reason I write poetry. It allows me to express myself and tell my story in a way that seems authentic to me. I genuinely hope that it helps others with similar experiences to feel encouraged and inspired in their own journey. I also find it helpful for myself because I believe that I'm doing something that may have a positive impact on others as well as attempting to break the stigma and encouraging empathy for individuals living with these experiences. We rarely get a back story from the media with a genuine narrative around these situations, especially when it comes to someone who has harmed. I guess it's hard to know what each individual is battling and how alone they may feel with that. Despite all the different stages, God has been the source of my recovery. Which is why I like to glorify him with my testimony.

As Jason says, we hope *The Burning Breath Chapters* brings something to the world which is much needed and of even greater use. Mase Okor's journey echoes the impact of a rippling pen in a similar way, as this young, accomplished writer tells us:

> I got into writing poetry in my final year of university. I wasn't pleased with the lack of diversity in our curriculum and decided to make a complaint about it. My then senior lecturer came back to me with this poetry collection called *Poor* by a British-Nigerian writer named Caleb Femi. I ordered the book and read it in an evening. I've always enjoyed storytelling and writing as a child and this invigorated that passion even more. Sharing similarities with Femi and the themes he writes about inspired me to get into writing. From there I started writing my own poems to eventually create my debut poetry collection *Sitting on the Sidelines*.
>
> Writing has been cathartic for me on a personal level. Getting to express my deepest thoughts on paper is a beautiful feeling. Ultimately it's a very vulnerable art form which has given me a strong sense of purpose, power, and self-worth.
>
> The arts can help solve problems faced in urban communities in multiple ways. Whether through writing poetry, music, or visual arts, the medium of the arts has the ability to bring people together. Having the place you grew up in represented in media can build a sense of community. Having a harrowing experience brought to life in the form of poetry can make you feel seen and heard. Music being played in a group setting can foster a sense of community and equalizes everyone to vibe to the rhythms and meaningful words.

In the vein of what Mase tells us, I have seen not just within myself but within the lives of people I work with, including close friends, this power the arts hold. My co-director Sean Perry, who helped to found my company Therapeutic Productions, has spoken publicly about how music gave him a lifeline whilst spending 15 years in the system, and just this year I began working with another man, who spent over 20 years in the system, who invited me to read his poetry collection, penned during his time inside, which saw him investigate himself, unveil the meaning of life, and cope in a situation many will never understand. We invite you to travel with our pens into waters that still the mind in a flow much the same as the current of a moving river.

This piece leans on and utilizes 28 case studies from frontline work in the criminal justice and mental health sectors whilst also using two in-depth case studies that explore the impact of mindfulness.

Our work centers on a journey through the stages of early childhood, adolescence, adulthood, and maturity, exploring the overcoming of traumatic experiences and adversities faced by those from urban communities. The writing has a focus on the practice and approach of mindfulness meditation and the incredible power of this form of therapy to transform the hearts of those who have found themselves at the edge of our society's experiences. A large part of the manuscript captures authoritative descriptions of life stages through a range of mindfulness textbooks by leading authors, case studies, leading works in philosophy, social sciences, Zen Buddhist theory, and psychology.

In addition to this, although descriptive nonfiction accounts provide a strong basis for our work, we have found that some experiences captured as case studies were best suited to creative expression to capture the intensity of experiences, emotions and insights, and so we have included factual poems that act as case study accounts of the life stages explored and the impact of mindfulness/Zen Buddhism. This also suits the context of the creative backgrounds of the authors.

As a result, the format of each chapter includes a descriptive account, an autobiographical account, followed by poetry, and concludes with recommendations to practitioners.

Acknowledgments

We would like to acknowledge Ron Maddox and Professor Kemmyo Taira Sato for providing insight and guidance in their meditative practice to our authors. We would also like to acknowledge Synergi Project, an organization that became the catalyst for this piece and has given much to survivors of prison and mental health systems. It is also important to acknowledge the board of directors of Unique Talent CIC and Therapeutic Productions CIC who have provided us with paths to reform and a wealth of guidance in assisting the lives of those at the margins of society. Lastly, we would like to acknowledge our service users and partners who we work with to make our corner of the world a better place.

Adolescence in the Hood

During the course of a person's life, the period known as adolescence (denoting a transition into adulthood) has great connotations for the shaping of a person's character. I have found that for many, this stage of life provides moments and lessons that can become determinants of a person's future. In the first part of this chapter, I would like to provide some insight into what I have found working with young people who are in this age group, as a means of assessing some of the challenges our communities face as well as homing in on our understanding of the different adolescent paths of some, which may require immediate intervention or diversion so that this does not inflict a negative effect on their trajectory in later years due to unresolved issues.

In parts of UK society, it is as though there are some who live in a totally different region of the world; the divergence of experiences is so wide that parts of the country appear like an isolated island. In my work I have spoken to young people taken into care in South London and groomed to strip and departmentalize ammunition, young men trained as specialists in the use of firearms in their early years. My company ran a media production course with sixth-form students based in the neighborhood I grew up in – Croydon, South London – back in 2021, and after we had interviewed 12 young people of all genders and many ethnicities, all of them recounted knowing people who were a part of the criminal world at the age of 17 or 18. For young women and young men, the issue of self-esteem, self-worth, and the need to prove oneself through violence or strength has ever been prevalent, but in some neighborhoods, I have seen firsthand and through my work how this is taken to the extreme. When I was growing up, from around the age of 14 carrying weapons and using weapons was a common characteristic of the kids in my year group at school, and this runs parallel to the experiences of young men I have worked with. A young man from Croydon, who I have worked with for over three years since he was in college, once spoke to me about the severe anxiety he was having growing up in a violent neighborhood and that he was at some points scared to travel and leave his house because of the amount of stabbings going on in his area. We spoke a great deal about how he felt the need to defend himself. For many young men caught carrying a knife, it is out of genuine fear for their safety on a daily basis, but in some parts of the political world this fails to gain recognition. In 2021, I attended a meeting where the Mayor's Violence Reduction Unit came to Croydon and we heard from a 12-year-old boy in Thornton Heath, South London, who challenged all of us in the room to question why it was that young people felt the need to carry a knife in the first place. It saddened me because he recounted an experience I faced over 15 years ago when I was his age; in many respects we faced the same issues.

In relation to this, I have delivered workshops to anti-knife campaigners called "The Climate of Fear," which summarizes the experience of many young people in British cities. In many respects this climate of fear is interwoven with extremes of toxic masculinity and desensitization, seen through my experience and observation at work; resulting in many young people feeling the need to be powerful. As a result, being violent and criminogenic is an expression of status and power. In 2022, my colleagues and I were delivering a presentation in Mitcham at a community center on a local estate when a young man we were working with spoke about how his criminal past was more extreme than the lives of many of the young people we were talking to at the time. Instantly, every one of the group of six young men in the community center protested about this with a great deal of pride and dismissive confidence. At the same time,

I opened up at this presentation about how my imprisonment had caused my mother great suffering, and the same group of young men laughed at this.

Over time, I had to learn within myself through harsh experiences that violence and strength are not worthy of validation and that defining strength must change in order to change attitudes and behavior. During my journey, mindfulness, through its emphasis on self-acceptance, was key to this. My experience was echoed when one of my mentees was remanded in custody and I went to visit him. This young man from Wandsworth, aged 17, opened up about being beaten in a fight in prison and talked me through his acceptance of this experience whilst not deflating his self-esteem. He also spoke about working with staff in prison around his emotions, and as someone who had known him for a year prior to this, I could see the maturity and change in him at this point.

Whilst I have begun this chapter with an exploration into a range of encounters with young lives, it is true that as an author I have direct experience of adverse conditions during adolescence. As an ex-offender I offer my life as an in-depth case study so that we can delve deeper into adolescent conditions among those from communities such as mine; as both an explanation of contributory factors that caused my incarceration in later life and as an example of the need for early intervention to ensure our youth have a quality of life. In the quote below from my autobiography you will find a descriptive account of my own challenges.

Excerpt from *Do You Have What It Takes?* — uncut edition by Jerome Sewell

From the age of 14, when I learnt that I did not have the courage to use weapons against the gangs attacking me in my local area, I relived conflict after conflict I found myself in at that age in my mind (ruminating over this as a teenager); 'what could I have done differently?' 'How could I have fought back?' *"I used to break up fights in school and adopted the martial art code from an early age; to be a defender of peace and justice and to build a more peaceful world"* I told the assistant psychologist who wrote a report about me in hospital. My mind is now thrown back to my days as a 9 year old, when I was in my local taekwondo school run by a traditional teacher of the Korean art of taekwondo. We stood in a uniformed line and I raised my hand with other students swearing an oath that would define some years of my childhood, when pledging allegiance to the Taekwondo tenets: 'courtesy' 'integrity' 'perseverance' 'self-control' and 'indomitable spirit'.

But from those days as a 9 year old, in comparison to the time when I was a teenager at the age of 14; when the tyrants of the gang world of London pursued me, I later would learn when in hospital as an adult that those tyrants not only won the battle against me when I was 14 years of age (by making me a victim physically), but to some extent they had won the war against me by determining my future and triggering the thought process that led to my incarceration. As a teenager I fought and fought my natural temperament; endowed with calmness and hated my weakness, lack of ability to fight back and lack of ability to feel strong. I was so desperate to be something I was not. My kung fu master said to me at the age of 21 *"you are either born a fighter or something makes you that way; fighting is something inside of you"*. For me something made me a fighter.

Whilst as authors we are happy to share accounts of our own lives and life stages through description, we have also found that as a means of exploring the range of emotions this stage in life can bring, poetry is the best method of communicating that side of our experience. The following poems in this chapter provide our exploration of this aspect of life.

Where Were You?
by Jerome Sewell

Where were you?
I couldn't find you,
The cub mounts his claws on a cliff,
For he faces horizons alone,
Solitude,
Fire, brimstone falling,
Moments erupting,
Flames
surround him,
Where were you?
Solitude,
Scars on my back,
Cut by knives,
Right before small eyes,
Swells on my face,
Taken to a hidden place,
Where were you?
I will face this,
I will not run from this,
Strong against odds,
I will face this,
Will they see me?
The surface in sight,
Holding me,
without insight,
They question me as the cause,
I am the effect,

I told you they were after me,
Where were you?
Held in places reckoned as soil,
Soil growing young roots,
But they left me here to die,
I made choices,
Choices to survive,
I must fight,
Sword, hammer and knife,
For you were never there for me,
You said you were my teacher,
my father, my elder,
I know only solitude,
My chest thunders,
I will hold on to this,
I will take this,
I will fly above this.
Lone hiker,
A torment of 100 pasts,
Home, playgrounds,
concrete jungles underneath stars,
Where were you?
Cultivation,
I am the becoming,
Threats made me,
I cannot stop,
Stop surviving,
But I am the becoming,
For once,
when alone,
I am happy,
Silence feeds every part of me,
The waters beckon me,
The texture of trees speaks to me,

Where were you?
I do not need you,
I do not hate you,
It is what it is,
I am what I am,
Gently, bring myself back,
Trembles,
Shaking my chest.

I have arrived now,
I am softened,
stronger now,
Melting an icing heart,
Solitude,
Quiet mind,
quiet in this life,
Stilled,
At ease,
ease amidst scattering,
Brought back by presence,
It is what it is,
I am where I am,
the now,
But where were you?
Moments captivate,
what seems 100 years of peace,
Just some space,
Watching water,
light moving across surfaces,
reminded of old encounters,
the monk and the girl in a garden,
Voicing thoughts,
The old man calls for silence,
'Just look.'

Isolation
by Jason Harris

It's hard to make people understand something that they choose not to
What is funny is that sometimes these same people will say don't worry I got you
which leaves me thinking, in what way?
when my things get tough, your presence starts to fade?

I get it and I know my reality may come across strange.
But all I am really trying to do is find the cause or a reason that explains.
By removing yourself, it leads to me thinking you're partly to blame
Although you're probably not, the mind likes to play its games

I am hearing voices and threats literally driving me insane.
Stuck in my house watching the cameras all day.
So cautious of my surroundings that loneliness has started to feel safe.
Frustrated by voices commenting on what I do or say.

Losing the will to do anything whilst trying to conceal the rage.
The people I come across judging by their expressions seem fake.
Pretending to understand but dismissive of all my claims.
Just feels like you're repeating the same cycle all over again.

Which makes seeking help seem pointless.
I'm now assuming everyone's the same.
Scared of how others may view me.
I cling to isolation to avoid the pain!

AL(LIEN) ONE
by Mase Okor

All alone, my mind a UFO glides, hurdles along in obsidian
sky aimlessly — Panning and probing, Waiting to see who
really sees me.

Lost.

Unidentified.

Misunderstood.

Constantly craving a connection.
I'm longing for your days, longing for your presence — like a
calendar with endless dates, but nothing is in place.
I'm waiting on that call, that text, the coincidental chance we
bump into each other again. I'm longing for the adrenaline
when my eyes meet yours.
I reminisce on those summer evenings when I didn't realise
how good I had it. I long for those mesmerising days and
endless nights.
I need you, I need me. You changed me, you saved me — you
gave me a release words can't describe. Just being real, I miss
our vibe.

Having looked at examples of young lives, personal experiences, and expressions concerning this stage in life, you may find that consistent themes are experiences of isolation, conflicting emotions, and trauma as a result of intense life experiences. Often, we may find when someone is going through this that it is having healthy relationships with people around them that can provide vital support. For social workers, offender managers or others working with adolescents who have been through adverse experiences, the relationship with their service user forms a firm basis for support that could be of great assistance to the youth they are working with. Using this as our foundation, in the final part of this chapter we will provide recommendations on how to build healthy professional relationships with service users.

Relationship Building for Service User Support

Building a relationship where people feel comfortable to share and become "weak" in front of you is important. Often, these relationships are built over time and people have to go through their own process; this is fundamentally about building trust. Many practitioners try to extract information and then, when this information is not readily available, accusations are made about the person being "guarded." But why exactly should anyone feel entitled to another person's information? Why exactly should someone have to provide information to you? Is it not their information? A job title does not make you a trusted person. There are times when young people have confided in me, giving information concerning their lives; there are some who have told me about terminal illnesses their family members are going through; others have cried to me over the phone; some have told me about distress at home. All of these situations were different but what was common was that person not only trusting me but in most cases seeing me as someone who cares about them. And this is echoed through my experiences in hospital. I would cite three or four key practitioners I trusted and who truly helped me, and in the case of those I am mentioning, that trust came from the fact that I observed their actions towards me, listened to how they spoke to me, and could plainly see they were going out of their way to help me. Often, it is not what is said, it is what people see in your actions which inspires trust. Empowering language does go a long way; taking the effort to see someone as an individual also goes a long way in this respect, as well as noting personality traits. One of my probation officers did this with me, when on one occasion I contested something we were speaking about and she turned to me and said that if I did not challenge the things she said this would be out of character for me.

Many professionals in this line of work engage in interviews and verbal communication with service users, and during these encounters, keeping people up to date, sharing opportunities with them, being non-judgmental, being compassionate (in the sense of empathy), avoiding harshness, being understanding, gentle, respectful, appreciative, and relating to people's struggles and weaknesses can help to facilitate a successful relationship. As an example of this, during the time I resided in supported accommodation in 2020, a key worker told us as residents about her diagnosis of depression, which inspired a great deal of respect for her. I would also add to this non-exhaustive list that letting someone know you are there for them, letting someone know this work is about them, actively listening, being accepting in some cases of a person's own ways of doing things, adapting to needs, and shaping your service around all of the aforementioned is also important.

The Struggle of Early Years

More and more emphasis at this point in society is being put on people's family life and the role of family instability as a core factor in the lives of young offenders. This emphasis appears to have come from a need to find the root causes of issues. Having begun our service user journey by focusing on adolescence as a core part of this life journey, we would now like to turn our attention to early life.

My company Unique Talent CIC over four years ago recognized the need for parents themselves to receive mentoring as well as their children, and as someone holding responsibilities for monitoring and collating the data in our organization, both in one-on-one conversations with mentors and in team meetings, I have heard of mentors needing to instigate family mediation to resolve issues in homes (including domestic abuse on some occasions). One young man from South London, who was designated a child in need, discussed being unhappy in the home due to family issues and it appeared to correlate with antisocial behavior he would instigate outside of the home. There have also been other young people whose support around drug use and other things has been intimately interwoven with their family life. In my line of work I have seen a growth in more support services for mothers and families as a whole in response to this component of a holistically seen problem. On some occasions I have applied for funding with these groups.

There are a multitude of issues young people can face in homes that impact their emotional, psychological, and financial situation. I remember when working on a film in 2022 that one young man from Mitcham, aged 19, opened up to me about him being the only support for his mother, which caused issues with his attendance at work, and some of my longstanding mentees have spoken to me of their fathers being imprisoned. Others have expressed how they missed having older siblings and father figures. The range of these experiences and responses to them can impact the developmental growth of young people, of course. I have colleagues who were high-level gang members who have stated that their main ambition was to take their mothers out of a council estate, which became a motivation for crime.

Often, there can be a focus on hard skills (such as employment), but we miss the fact that far more fundamental is someone's processing of information, analytical skills, problem-solving skills, and emotional intelligence; all of which are the foundations of all other skillsets and are directly linked to an aptitude for hard skills. I have worked with longstanding partners such as Bettering Education in Croydon who have published White Papers on the link between soft skills and employment rates among people from deprived social economic backgrounds (Health Foundation, *Improving Health Outcomes of Young People by Developing Soft Skills*, 2017). In my work as a service manager for Home-Start in Haringey, Hackney, and Waltham Forest, I worked with an organization that focused on providing support for families with young children. During my training with this organization it was emphasized that the main way children learn is through playing in the home environment; this is only one example of how the home impacts those overlooked skillsets that determine how young people face challenges and interact with the world. In a recent documentary drama I made about mental health, in 2024, a young man from Croydon said that often it is not the situation itself but how you respond to a situation that is important; decision-making again being a soft skill that determines how well we handle problems and move forward with our lives. Mindfulness shaped my thought processes, helping me to make better decisions and think clearly in order to engage in skillful actions.

My home life in many ways demonstrates issues that can shape the minds of young people growing up in communities such as mine, and in the end, mindfulness repaired much of the damage this caused me. For our assessment of early life I have again provided my own story as a case study.

Excerpt from *Do You Have What It Takes?* – uncut edition by Jerome Sewell

I was born in my grandmother's house to a mother who didn't know much of the world. I grew up with her in a council flat for most of my life, up until I turned 18. There are [a lot] of memories I have in that council flat and a lot of experiences; like old friends I met as a child whose weddings I attended later on in life. But there were also deep scars.

When my step father went to prison, my father was taken from me and a hole was left in a child's life. Looking back, I have become aware in the work that I do of the immense amount of experience I have in life, particularly in regards to the suffering of those less fortunate in our society; the ones who they say life dealt a bad hand.

I had tremendous affection for him (he truly was the father I would have always dreamt of). It is perhaps true to say that I have never felt a stronger bond with any man other than him; he was kind and humble. This is the story of the young bloods of South London. As a child I remember reading his letters from prison and seeing photos of him; I'll never forget the first time I picked up the phone to hear his voice again. It may have been awkward but he still called me son over the line.

You may be asking where my dad was at this point; most of the time he was around and we spent weekends together. My dad has always been a tough guy; good with his fists, polite and nice by nature but very rough around the edges (a genuine geezer with a good heart). I never felt close to him, not like my stepfather; I always felt distant and disconnected from him and I didn't have much respect for him because I simply didn't like him that much. At the age of 14, after we had an argument; when I was rude (in his view) over the phone, he took me below a restaurant and beat me into the ground and kicked me against the floor. Years later, I sat there as a 27 year old man in a forensic hospital, finally realising that he actually abused me at that age rather than what my family seemed to see it as; which is as just an extension of our Caribbean culture and the way things were done. I told him when I left hospital "you abused me", he turns back to me "[you're] just playing the victim". I write this with great sadness, to know that your father thinks that your realisation that you were abused as a child is pretending to be a victim.

Anyway a number of these men were my icons and influences, in addition to my uncles and other members of my family; some who helped to cushion me. Despite what I have said, my childhood was still full of happy memories but it is right to be mindful of the bad times and what was wrong.

Apart from the men in my life, there were other strains and tremendous tribulations my family faced as time went on.

Taking the perspective that early life provides the root of a person's character and experiences, and taking the perspective that it is a deciding cause of whether a person is capable of weathering and dealing with their challenges, this life stage provides the basis for both a healthy adulthood and a happy youth. At times when undergoing issues at a young age, due to the lack of development of communication skills it can be hard to articulate the feelings and thoughts of that stage in life. The poems in this next part of our chapter will be helpful in bringing these experiences to life in a bigger way.

Burning Breath
by Jerome Sewell

He stands in the dark of night,
shadow cast downwards,
luminescent like moonlight,
floods open to overwhelming sorrow,
his heart leaking, sore, an aching wound; soft and tender,
penetrative and deep,
As dark thoughts overtake him,
Floodgates pouring,
His mind recoils into prayer;
Prayers celestial in standing,
Lifting thoughts to high heaven,
Demons erupt in clouds,
Light glistens from his white gown;
knees touching the ground, head bowed,
So he recoils,
fastened in focus to heaven,
'Oh God, please give me strength, for my soul cries out to you.'
Thoughts hold his throat,
like the choke of a strangler,
His brother screams; howling,
His mother's tears, desperate,
Where will they go?
Decrees echoing,
For the son must lead his pack,
As an old lion is flung into burly dungeons,

Belmarsh,
Visions juxtaposing against life,
They pursue him,
and blackened night overshadows his young form,
Times of villains, glory, war and bloodshed,
Amidst burning fire,
Gangland conflict,
On days he sits,
Amidst stories of hood legends;
Young days of reckless thefts, untold crime,
New to moments,
Letters from old fathers, stained by cells.

Moments sow time,
They travel,
His incarceration,
Misery and despair amidst Love,
Broken hearts,
Pain and bereavement,
The devil's game.
Smoke of a past clears into sight,
A mind's eye revealing drug dealers,
They threaten his family,
Caged,
Bleeding pain from veins cut,
Opened by a cruel world,
Memory after memory takes hold,
Robes become whiter,
Prayers are firmer,
A Muslim scholar once said:
'There were men in the hadith that in times of war even when arrows would go through their skin would not break the focus of their prayers.'
Desperation increases,

And so his hymns;
Salvation,
Only among those at the mercy of their sustainer,
'They say it is to Allah that we belong and to Allah that we will return.'
'Know that I am the lord and be still.'

Distant in impression.
Deep in meditation,
Mind stilled and body folded,
A realm where dimensions of time slow,
I find myself resonating,
penetrating peace,
thoughts inwardly silent,
a comfort within stills my soul,
putting me at ease within,
an ease not felt within weeping trembles that troubled me,
quelled with numb drugs,
As I sit, thoughts move,
appearing, ricocheting and speeding across blackened space,
An immovable stone grounding me,
anchoring my focus,
Each thought moved,
cut downwards by swords guarding my mind,
in the silence of the moment;
a silence as deep as the endless oceans,
each intruder imposing on sacred grounds,
swiftest attack,
My mind is the katana of life.

Do you feel I earned my rank?
Did I fight for a just cause?
A cause decided by heaven,
far above me;

Destroying confines,
Releasing relentless light,
It breaks through,
Zen is destructive,
meditation is destructive,
The monk penned,
And so fire surrounds Fudo Myoo,
fire breaks my admitted cage,
tearing, crumbling fetishes,
in a material life,
inwardness, 'immovable' in distant impression.

To conclude this chapter, having found that a consistent theme depicted in the previous chapters has been instability and toxicity in the environment, this leads us conveniently into the subject of how we create environments for our service users as professionals. As all too often I have seen alternative spaces outside of damaging ones become spaces of refuge, particularly for the youngest.

Practice in the Home Environment

When it comes to matters in the home, professionals can have a range of functions, such as helping to support families by accessing services that will enhance the financial or social situation of the entire household (social workers often take on such a function). However, what may be missed is that as professionals we facilitate the creation of a space that may provide a cushion for chaotic and damaging events experienced elsewhere in our service users' lives. At work, I have taken part in funding panels which have worked to fund organizations providing mental health support for ethnic minorities, and what struck me whilst reviewing over 20 funding applications is the range of community facilities that are creating safe spaces across the UK for people, and often these spaces can be found in a variety of settings such as churches, community centers, or even musical shows; but what they have in common is providing a network of individuals that provide support. In 2021, I attended a presentation when the Contextual Safeguarding model was becoming popular and a professor spoke of those who groom and exploit young people as being very effective at drawing people in by capitalizing on qualities (such as excitement) that match developmental emotional needs of adolescents. This is whilst local authority services are completely the opposite much of the time, in respect of being seen as dull and boring. As a qualified youth worker, I learned early on in my studies of Youth Work with Need2Suceed (my course provider) that it is also a developmental factor for adolescents to gravitate towards peer groups and away from the home environment. For my own part, I have mentioned damaging experiences in my home environment, and in my youth this caused me to gravitate to other spaces which could fill emotional voids; some of these places were unhealthy such as older friends who I would smoke with, and some were healthy places, like mentors and other family members' homes.

As a professional, providing a service may be the objective (irrespective of what our fields or professions are), but service delivery takes place within a space. During the making of films, I often work with people on mobile film sets across London, but the space itself, which is usually filled with people, can create an impact due to interpersonal factors. For example, when I reported the impact of one of my projects, I noted that our film sets facilitated networks of young creatives meeting each other and supporting each other, according to the accounts of those I worked with. We should think to ourselves: what type of space am I creating? How will I deliver this service and what space is conducive to delivering this service? Often this can come down to the people involved in our interventions, whilst some use sights and sounds. My company Therapeutic

Productions led an intervention based on heritage and black history whilst collaborating with the Museum of London in 2024. When we took our young people to the Museum, the staff there delivered a workshop in collaboration with the mental health charity Mind that involved exploring the transatlantic slave trade through objects and artifacts but also through the use of spices and smells which represented products related to the trade of enslaved Africans. Whilst in hospital, I myself took part in a modern board-games group run by an occupational therapist, who in one of her sessions utilized a Japanese theme where she provided wasabi peas and sushi and decorated the room. I noted in a magazine that her group provided one of the most positive environments during my admission. These examples demonstrate that engagement tools that provide excitement and at times (particularly when career orientated) aspiration can facilitate growth. On one occasion I spoke to a youth worker whilst delivering a presentation at a community center in Wandsworth and said to him that we are a part of the same movement and he responded by stating that he doesn't have thousands of pounds backing him (which was referenced against my fundraising history). But I would contest that our community centers in local areas have the ability to become high-quality provision services; as the secret of good provision isn't necessarily money — it is innovation and ideas that stretch the imagination (alongside the use of interests and passions). Working with skilled people who can bring these things to life is often enough.

Cultural competence, sights and sounds, but above all else welcoming environments that stimulate and interest are the crucial factors behind everything mentioned here. This applies to the space and the delivery which takes place in the space. During mentoring it is often purely conversations based on interests that create a stimulating environment, but I would add that, at times, vision, big thinking, aspiration, the practicality of making a vision a reality, and getting people to join networks, groups and ecosystems (so that they bounce off each other) are marks of high-quality provision.

Mindfulness, as we will see in subsequent chapters, relies, some might say, on the premise that we use tools at our disposal (i.e. our own bodies) to create a safe space of awareness and reflection for ourselves; I have heard some teachers mention the idea of our breathing exercises being like the inside of a ship amidst rocky waves, giving us stability amidst a chaotic mind. When I remember back, I barely had any one-on-one conversations with my first meditation teacher but he created a space where insight could reach me. In the same vein, as practitioners, our spaces have the ability to create conducive conditions for healing; this is not determined by the nature of the space but what we create with our space from what we have, and how we create spaces shaped around the comfort of our service users.

Reckless Days of a Teenage Wildness

Returning to the topic of adolescence, we have found it necessary to follow up on this life stage by emphasizing some behaviors we may see adolescents take on when traumas and instability necessitate coping mechanisms. This takes us into the following narrative concerning drug and alcohol addiction.

In the UK, and particularly in London, young people face many rites of passage into adulthood: for some this could be getting a car or going to university, but for many others, having your first drink or having your first smoke of weed may mean graduation into adulthood. For many, these things are part and parcel of youth, but what we later realize is that a great deal of things around us promote unhealthy lifestyles. We see this through the most primary needs we have, such as fast-food shops that are now stopping deliveries to schools; or the bigger things, such as smoking cigarettes being banned in public places. Many of these societal changes could be looked at as shifts out of an unhealthy lifestyle that has been conveniently placed at easy access to us. However, the record number of those facing drug and alcohol addiction (for example, the number of adults entering treatment for substance misuse in 2022–2023 was 137,749, according to reports from the Office of Health Improvement and Disparities) tells us slightly more about the conditions of British society, with many perhaps finding a need for escapism; but escaping from what? For many youth, it may be a case of trying to escape at times from living conditions that young lives are not meant to cope with. Dialectical Behavioral Therapy refers to adaptive and maladaptive coping strategies ("21 Emotion Regulation Worksheets & Strategies," *Positive Psychology*, 2018), and for many, drug and alcohol use becomes a destructive coping strategy because you are finding escapism in something that is destroying you.

Apart from spending time in prison, I have spent time on three psychiatric wards holding approximately ten people at a time. As you would expect, I have spent time speaking to many of the men I resided with, and every single one of them spoke of having addiction to some form of drug, or having alcohol addiction. A good friend of mine wrote an account of his life called *Once Upon a Time in Brixton* which explained how he fell into crack cocaine addiction and the impact this had on his mental health (Kray Matt, Tim Pritchard, and Wayne Hutchinson, *Once Upon a Time in Brixton*, 2021). Then, in the work that I do, many young men have used drugs. There are many debates on all of this, but having lived and worked around this for a long time now it becomes harder to deny the link between addiction and mental health issues. When going to live in supported accommodation in 2020, I witnessed men getting addicted to cannabis, and one of them turned to me and admitted he had fallen into addiction. In this context, many fail, I think, to understand the nature of addiction; people sometimes see addiction as a choice between strength and weakness when in reality I have seen and spoken to some men who simply cannot escape demons in their past. They are running away from memories and fall back into drug use because the root cause has not been addressed. One of the men who lived next to me in the hostel I was sent to in 2020 used to shout and scream into the night out of anguish; on one occasion, I was in our communal kitchen cooking and he recounted a story to me of when he was 6 years old in Jamaica (which is where he was born) screaming because of starvation and hunger, and I finally grasped a small insight into what he was battling. At one stage he asked if I thought we were meant as people to suffer.

In my practice of mindfulness, I learned a number of things that gave me adaptive or positive coping strategies, and mindful meditation was one of them itself. I was able to gently be at peace with myself, with my own thoughts and feelings, especially when alone. This was partly through acceptance but also by that creation of a distance from your thoughts that mindfulness encourages. One of the most profound lessons that my first meditation teacher taught me in 2019 was that I am not my thoughts. The root of this teaching is deeply Buddhist in nature, some might say: encouraging detachment from the ego, the concept of self, or the "I" as it is called, and removing that individuality which attaches us to what we feel. Whilst in hospital I would simply sit in bed and not do anything and be with any thoughts and feelings that came. What I found through meditation is not only that I enjoyed the silence itself but also that I actually enjoyed the removal of unhealthy habits and becoming healthier in my lifestyle.

As a youth I was with a friend from West Africa and we were drinking together; then he recounted how he watched an albino man get killed in front of him during the civil war in his home country because the soldiers wanted to see if he had magic powers because of his skin tone. I remember understanding after this why he used to drink so heavily and I recognized that need to run away…

The issues covered above demonstrate the relationship between cause and effect in adolescent lives. Below, when reading the autobiographical quote provided by myself, it is important to connect this with my aforementioned experiences in the previous chapters as they are interconnected.

Excerpt from *Do You Have What It Takes?* by Jerome Sewell

> Those were the days [where] I would chill with my older friends in Kingston upon Thames, smoking weed all night in the studio and making music; spitting over rap beats. Those college times in west London with the other students; in a park smoking a bong and getting fucked out

of my head, smoking high grade with a Rasta and zoning out. Back in those days I was with my cousin [a lot] from east London, I was the calm one and he was wild as hell. I remember when he and I went to [Crystal Palace] for my 17th birthday, booked a hotel room and smoked £50 worth of weed by ourselves and steamed the night out. Then I was dancing with 18 year olds in house raves in Acton. 'There were so many parties', my boy Ben said [to me] 10 years later. My friends and I used to meet every weekend to figure out the motive; I was the man back in the day at the age of 16 cruising through London with 25 year olds in cars, older men who [saw] me as [their] younger brother. Just like the time I arranged a DJ gig for a party for a girl at my school, took my £10 cut from the DJ, ended up in London [B]ridge meeting my cousin from east London and then we travelled back to the house of my 'olders' in Kingston; entering a rap battle scene in their house. We took a few drinks, then a spliff and then we were taken in a friend's car to a house rave in Purley where my cousin and I were dancing with 25 year olds; holding [their] backsides against our waist. Or what about the time I was smoking a massive tulip (a spliff formed of 15 [Rizlas] made into a massive ball), smoking it like an engine exhaust pipe with steam like a chimney coming out from my mouth. Who amongst us forgets [their] first-time smoking weed and drinking at the same time? I left a barbecue in Kingston; stoned and drunk, meeting my friends at East Croydon train station and entering with them to a rave in central London. I found myself dancing with 10 girls and getting at least 4 numbers that night. Then there was the time we were in Vauxhall and I was pinned against a wall as a girl span herself against me. Those were the days.

In the midst of the London riots of 2010, I was with one of my girlfriends in Thornton [H]eath; I still call her the temptress to this day. I recollected those days to my friend Wayne in hospital whilst asking if he ever had sex whilst high on weed before, remembering when my ex blew smoke into my mouth. That girl was trouble; getting me into fights [where] guys wanted to brick my head in. As I got older my life's need for experiences increased; from clubbing in [Bar Rumba] to those days whilst I was at university with my half Jamaican and Irish friend, drinking [absinthe] in a bar in Shoreditch and [losing] my mind; smacking a [woman's] backside and blacking out on the floor. What of the happy hours at Las Iguanas in Spitalfields; spending hundreds of pounds on alcohol and drinking cocktail jugs of [Long Island] ice tea. To times with my [Sierra] Leonean friend who took me to African raves; he was my drinking buddy, constantly loading me up with Guinness at wedding receptions.

When bringing us to the next phase of our current chapter, in the sense of emotive poetry, you may find below the wrapping of intense feelings and emotions in regard to addictions and harmful substance abuse, bringing us to certain conclusions concerning these experiences.

Drunken Pain
by Jerome Sewell

The bottle doesn't end,
And there are no ends to its shades,
Just two men,
Just two hearts,
Bullets,
Showering over covers,
wrapped in sweat,
Firm,

lustful to touch,
Far far away,
But so near,
Moments found,
Amidst a life we must all live,
Where were you?
Just two men drinking,
Will we lose the world?
They cut him,
Rusting blades opening up,
The spell is broken,
Eyes snap open,
To a new world,
In a land far far away,
Far from tropical planes,
But somewhere so close,
As close as concrete jungles,
Just two men,
Two men drinking,
Glory amidst a blaze of conflict,
A reckless wind,
The darkness,
The unbecoming,
Just two men,
Holding bottles to jaws,
Just two men,
Sinking under a cause,
Is health wealth?
He asks himself,
Will I love myself before this ice melts?

Following the themes of this chapter, our last section concerns alternative views on how to address drug and alcohol addiction relevant to both the life stage itself and the noted thread concerning maladaptive coping strategies. This includes our role as professionals in addressing this with our service users.

Drug and Alcohol Interventions During Practice

Often, when people face addiction, during admission to a hospital they may undergo CBT (Cognitive Behavioral Therapy), and having participated in around six sessions of this myself, I experienced there being many sessions where we would write down different strategies and many different forms of tuition about thoughts and cycles of thinking. However, at this point in my journey I had given up smoking weed (my drug of choice) almost two years before through the method of going "cold turkey" in prison. But what I had not given up was smoking cigarettes, and going from a prison, where smoking was permitted, into a psychiatric hospital where it was banned, I knew this was the addiction that I needed to fight at that stage. In the early days of my admission, my frequency of smoking (which was hourly) was replaced with drinking cups of tea hourly. The staff on the acute ward I was admitted to eventually dubbed me the "tea champion" because of this. Drinking tea curbed the smoking for me due to replacement; it was perhaps the first step in heading towards a healthier lifestyle, and when all is said and done, it does come down to lifestyle. To illustrate this point, I remember as a teenager, as I was getting more into smoking marijuana, I had a close friend who was a footballer and he decided to cut down at this time. In this way his career was shaping him to live a healthier life, and this experience was echoed years later when one of my colleagues referred me to a weightlifter who wanted help raising finance for a community initiative teaching power-building to youth. He called his gym his "church" in our first conversation.

Often, living a healthy lifestyle requires a motivating factor and enjoyment found in healthy activities. Hospital admissions for forensic service users often result in permission to use leave to engage with the community and phase back into society. At this stage, one has access to a number of free services; this is how I discovered not only mindfulness but also reiki and many other therapies (which became my longstanding adaptive strategies for positive emotional release). Many young people use music for this purpose; one young man from Wandsworth spoke to me of using music to explore his emotions after he left prison. My company Therapeutic Productions runs interventions where we make films and our cast and crew take part in drama therapy exercises during rehearsals. We ran these sessions consistently with a group of six youth who were from a council estate, and during monitoring reviews some youth stated that the session revealed to them how enjoyable therapy could be. This was an example of how bringing new strategies and coping tools for mental health to communities can allow people to test and learn new methods of healing. Some methods are also self-taught (like prisoners serving life sentences who I have worked with who took up writing poetry about their life experiences).

As professionals, building our referral processes to bring new methods to people is helpful. At a social work conference in 2024 I spoke about a number of ways practitioners can help service users in forensic units to engage in art, which included:

1. Covering capital costs for software and equipment in conjunction with the occupational technicians and finding ways they can access old equipment they have had previously
2. Liaising with family to get access to someone's material
3. For those who have leave, finding community resources that focus on their artistic work
4. Monetization of artistic material for income through streaming and online methods of making money

5. Skills-based training inside the hospital and working with external providers
6. Focusing on their goals

It is also true that we can make a concerted effort to organize our own service delivery. In my own practice I found that I could refer a theatrical service to a young man who went to prison, an example of why we need to build partnerships and take a lead in organizing delivery through co-production and collaboration, notwithstanding our primary function.

Crime Sagas

This manuscript takes us through a life journey analysis of life stages and now at this point we reach the stage of committing a criminal offense. Due to the case study approach, we highlight offenses committed in adulthood, but we hope readers appreciate that we are not isolating our analysis to just this context of offending, which can of course happen at almost any stage of a person's life. What we seek at this point is to provide a distinct analysis in the following account.

Over time I have met many people who have committed many types of offenses. My favorite philosopher from the European Enlightenment, Richard Price, wrote that when a person commits an evil act it is often the result of the accumulation of many evil acts over the course of their life (*Principal Questions in Morals*, 1758, 3rd ed. revised 1787). Separating ourselves from the word "evil," I must say that I have generally found the concept he espoused a common theme. When Price was describing this, he was indicating that often a crime that comes before the courts is one major act that has taken place due to a buildup of negative conduct over years. Often a criminal offense is the tip of the iceberg, and underneath are many habits and smaller acts that have built up to this. I have found in my own case and the case of others I have spoken to that, before being convicted of a crime, for many years before this there has often been the perpetrating of smaller antisocial acts which someone was not caught for. There are many elements to a crime and this is reflected in our laws when the term "intention" and others like it are used. As much as a person's act of choosing to have children has many causes and surrounding circumstances, the act of committing an offense also has many parts to it. In the criminal justice system, when someone is assessed by the probation system there will often be discussion over their risk factors and protective factors; whilst in forensic psychiatry, great time is taken in assessments to look at all elements of a person's life. This follows an increasing need to be holistic in our understanding of someone's behaviors and predicting someone's eventualities. At 117 discharge meetings (which are formal meetings held before someone is discharged from hospital) a person's social life, family life, employment, financial circumstances, housing circumstances, personal relationships, mental health diagnosis, along with a host of other things, are pulled into question.

Going back to the conversation on soft skills from previous chapters, another set of characteristics overlooked is people's morality, which is deeply related to their decision-making. A person's beliefs (spiritual or otherwise) and value systems can at times be some of the most fundamental influences on rehabilitation and offending. There is a popular opinion that draws on the link between low educational attainment and crime (for example, the report *The Links between Young People Being Imprisoned, Pupil Background and School Quality* published by the Office for National Statistics in 2023 draws this correlation), but this is something that I have always had issues with. I was a university student when I committed my offense and I graduated before being sent to prison. I have also worked with young men who have been on probation licenses whilst studying at college and left with distinctions. Inside hospital and prison I spent time with men who had graduated from university; in fact a friend of mine who is a lived-experience practitioner not only had a degree but also worked on engineering airplanes before he was convicted. I fundamentally challenge the idea that academic education informs your value systems; it may very well influence your prospects but not necessarily your moral compass. There are studies about rational choice theory which people use as a formula for how people make decisions, stating in the context of offending that a crime is calculated to be worth the risk by an offender (Ally Fogg, *Let's Be Rational about Gangs*, 2008). But upon discharge I have worked with several men who have spoken of how easy it would be for them to make more money by returning to a life of crime but they choose not to, not because of the risk but because it has now become something fundamentally against their value systems.

When I was growing up, churches such as The Potter's House in Croydon took in many gang members who claimed to change their lives. In later years, SPAC Nation (whatever the controversy) would become another church in the UK that saw former gang members come and reform, as shown in news reports. The church teaches a certain value system whilst also providing a pro-social community in many cases, but it is that part of it, I would state – a teaching about morality – which becomes the defining factor for many of these gang members. It presents a different way of life and perspective on the world. In my work as a monitoring lead, mentors have spoken to me of cases where young men have found a resolve to live their lives differently due to an incident changing their perspective: sometimes they may be betrayed; other times they may choose to listen to a mentor and change their mind about getting the revenge they once wished to get (as in the case of a gang leader from Hounslow, West London, who one of our mentors worked with); or they may learn that a previous way of handling something isn't worth it. And it is that (a change in perspective) that many times changes behavior going forward. One of my colleagues described the birth of his daughter as being his motivating factor whilst he was a high-level founder of a gang based in South London.

For myself, the mindful practice of compassion, that gentle self-soothing attitude and perspective, along with my understanding of Zen philosophy regarding the nature of conditions conducive to my personal growth, was what changed my perspective...

In the quote below I provide some aspects that conclusively summarize my offending journey, emergence from this stage, and later realizations.

Excerpt from *Do You Have What It Takes?* by Jerome Sewell

In the month of April 2020, I stood as a guest speaker in front of the Recovery [C]ollege's class of ex-offenders who reside in a mental health institution; ready to tell my life story in the midst of an educational course that I developed for an institution that provides psychological education to ex-offenders who have been hospitalised because of mental disorders. I both originated the idea for this course and led the team in constructing it, named 'Perspectives of violence'. There were about 5 people there; which as far as courses for this type of cohort go was a healthy number. Before I arrived to deliver the course, on the way up to the venue, whilst on the bus I made some notes of what I was going to talk about. When we got to this part of the workshop, as I stood up my heart poured out.

Just to interject with some of my own thoughts about my offence: It's a funny thing, those moments of my life I will never forget. The evening was a dark, surreal episode of thriller movie type stuff. I left my house with a knife concealed in my long jacket, taken from the kitchen. I was pumped up on the sounds of dancehall artist 'Tommy Lee' listening to my favourite among his songs at the time (with a chorus that touched deep into my violent instincts) *"kill them allllllllllllllll!"* the artist sang as I walked to pursue the victim of a crime that would cause us both devastation in the future. I headed to another borough in London, travelling from the one I lived in; taking the tram and then catching a bus. I was in my second year of university then, studying film and broadcasting and it was on that day of the week I decided to execute a dangerous task.

Three years later, I would find myself in a white room with a psychologist inside a forensic hospital; asking me direct questions about how I would personally describe what psychologists call your 'drivers' and 'destabilisers' (which are psychological terms that refer to what drove you as an offender to commit an offence and what characteristics you have that made it likely you would offend) and I answered:

"I would say malevolent planning". The psychologist looked at me *"that's a strong way to describe yourself Jerome"*.

In the vein of the last phrase mentioned previously, "malevolent planning," violent ideation is a subject deserving of both depiction and recognition; the reform of a person's mind is something very personalized and intimate. In the following poems, that intimacy as found within a person's mental space is conveyed for our readers.

The Beast and the Garden
by Jerome Sewell

I will leave this place,
He will never see his loved ones again,
The voice of a demon,
Held behind cages,
The dragon swells in a chest,
Tumbleweed
gathers speed under oil,
Blazing to its destination,

Until sinking under depths,
Journey to the underworld,
Graduation,
From swings,
To a blaze,
To wounds,
I took this,
I will not take this,
I am not weak,
I am strong now,
I will rise now,
Greazy now,
It transforms heaven into hell,
Bodhi into delusion,
How can a Zen man assent to it?
Sokoto pens scribe,
Inking his heart.

Returning to the breath,
Eyes open,
Amidst gardens,
Gentle petals,
The enemy stands by the wayside,
You can run from yourself,
But you cannot escape your destiny,
Finding of the becoming,
Ease in,
Ease out,
I am myself,
Softer now, stronger now,
Free to be who I was always meant to be,
I became the man I was meant to become,
The sword is to give life,
Thoughts to high heaven,

Accepting,
I am me,
Holding my space,
Not so far away,
I am not my thoughts,
The descending,
Reaching planes,
Revealing a lifetime of mending,
Even if he returns 100 times,
Over 100 lives,
The ticking would weigh,
As if holding the balance of skies,
High heaven,
The surrender,
Depths,
Across rising colours,
Sprinkling life into petals,
Full of the living,
Transcending death,
Giving in,
ice within,
steaming by acceptance,
I am me,
That voice,
With a chamber of Truth,
I am not my thoughts,
I am my silence,
Soft to touch,
Harmony in stillness,
Harmony for a heavenly reason.
The straying mind
Holds nothing.
My skin
Crawls with foul senses,

Telling,
The reminding,
It is an imposter,
The old man breathes,
From veils of a hallowed place,
Telling you to abandon lies of a misled world,
The carpenter,
Enslaved,
Occupied,
In the face of a world that worships death,
Tells the fable of love,
As armies head towards hills,
Through deserts,
And dense lakes,
Beasts are made into men,
He lifts against the shadow of death,
High heaven.

And so a man witnesses the child,
Desperate for his place,
Air thickened with sweat and falseness,
Be himself,
Be yourself,
The chest falls back,
The struggle declines,
gardens transform inside,
Residing across rivers,
In landscapes,
In the reflection of a cup,
What, oh where is time?
They won the battle,
Will God win the war?
Shaking,
Breaking,

Unbecoming,
For a cub
must hold his skin under firmaments,
Rain and lightning,
Pain and loss,
Holding on to dust,
Until his last breath,
Blows into this garden,
The first stage of mindfulness is acceptance.

The core of this chapter has been reformation of the mind. A very delicate and complex theme. Charting this type of change is very difficult and almost always perhaps suited to a qualitative method that relies on depth. How a person reaches this point could be termed highly individualistic but, within this, encompasses our role as practitioners in assisting with this change. As a result, we decided to end this chapter with guidance for the role of practitioners in changing perspectives.

Changing Service User Perspectives During Practice

Changing someone's perspective – such a vital yet overlooked aspect and skillset. Apart from persuasion employed in corporate companies, we rarely hear of such a skillset being taught in the criminal justice or mental health sectors, but it is arguably this vital skill which makes many mentoring organizations such a strong asset. Organizations such as those I work with will argue to both funders and criminal justice workers that relationship building is the USP (Unique Selling Point) that enables them to reach the hardest-to-reach communities (such as high-risk offenders) and facilitate engagement among service users who frequently disengage with services. The aim of this relationship building is to leverage a bond to both advise and get through to someone, challenge perspectives, and create a space filled with support.

I was having a conversation with a former probation officer who was having issues when giving instructions to clients, and I referenced an experience I had when a young person's behavior at work needed to be questioned and, in this instance, immediately when I challenged his behavior, he said I was right to say the things I had said. In this and many other cases we see the power of relationships to create conducive conditions for changing behavior and actions.

From a mindful perspective, the creation of a space for reflection, a practice that brings clarity of thought and guidance underpinned by self-acceptance and your own inner value systems, is what is used to change behavior. Some call this "inquiry." Mindfulness teachers taught me that actually the practice of being still and observing thoughts has enough power in itself to give clarity that changes actions. There is a lot to learn from this approach: practitioners can create a space where someone's values are given motivation through this; interventions driven by accepting individuality and building on this. Mindfulness teachers also taught me at times without the use of one-on-one conversation and purely through a guiding voice in a group, accompanied by practical steps. Often, my method of teaching is similar: doing something with someone practically whilst providing guiding advice regarding their path. Changing perspectives often involves removing things that have distorted our perspective and morality, in addition to emotional, mental, and physical scars. Removing or healing these things can be difficult but from a mindful perspective can take place by removing the inner critic and by the practice of acceptance; allowing enough space to change things. To accept oneself means to be happy and to love oneself, and self-love I would argue is the root of making decisions that are right for oneself.

It is important for practitioners to address service users' personal problems with compassion, humanity and sympathy instead of using clinical methods or attacking them. This means staying away from formulas and just having real conversations based on experiences and based on compassion. In such a space, people can read the intention of a person and see their humanity. Many young people have said that they see me as the soft, compassionate, patient and accepting voice that they can listen to, someone who creates a space for growth and, importantly, the ability to accept the help offered. Such was the case for a young person on a media course who was consistently late and who I spoke to. At this point, after I spoke, he told me that I was the first person who had offered to help him with mistakes he was making rather than just tell him off. Much of this is based on the simple concept of being gentle and having compassionate, genuine intention when working with someone.

Falling into Psychosis

This next chapter covers a stage that many ex-offenders will not directly face, in that the development of acute disorders falls into a wider scope of causality including brain development, workings of the mind, and other things. However, to provide and cater for the breadth of professional roles and encompass all sides of our lived experience, we have decided to dedicate a chapter to this, beginning with the descriptive account below.

Hearing voices, seeing things that don't exist… those who study this may just see them as things that are uncommon experiences, but truly, psychosis will make a person question the subject of metaphysics or the nature of reality (even if you are unlike me who just has an inherent interest in these things); after all, what is real and what is not real could be considered one of those all-encompassing questions of life itself. During my work for the Royal College of Psychiatrists I have often spoken up about the lack of cultural insight into what psychosis looks like for Afro-Caribbean people in comparison to other cultures, since the Mental Health Act Review of 2018 cited the issue of disproportionate numbers of black people being sectioned. For many children growing up in Afro-Caribbean households, supernatural occurrences may be deemed to be a part of their culture; if you were to walk into a Pentecostal church you might find cases of demon possession with people shaking on the ground having fits and people speaking in unknown languages with eyes closed, claiming to have the power of an essentially invisible force speaking through them (this is called "speaking in tongues"). This is also true of other cultures' experiences. In religious texts we read stories of men seeing angels with five heads on a chariot of fire – in the Book of Ezekiel for example – and if a person walked up to a psychiatrist and said they had experienced this, alongside other experiences in the Scriptures, I wonder what would be said about them?

I used to have a Rastafarian friend in hospital who said he would one day die and come back to life, and we spoke a great deal about spiritual things. On one occasion he came back from a meeting with the clinical team furious about the fact that the doctor accused him of engaging in pseudo-philosophy. This was what his spiritual expression was termed as. In truth, was he making up philosophy or was he exploring concepts and ideas foreign to a Eurocentric interpretation of the world? Given the fact that this man read texts on Egyptology and Afrocentric spirituality. When leaving hospital, I engaged and worked with a professor at King's College London who introduced me to the concept of "narrative therapy," based on the premise that we are the stories we tell ourselves and the stories other people tell about us, according to what she said. Later on, in 2021, I would deliver a narrative therapy-based intervention called "The Tree of Life" with a hospital and a group of service users. This intervention was based on the African concept of a tree in Zimbabwean culture and exploring what parts of a tree relate to different parts of our lives. Storytelling in the form of artistic depictions predates civilization, judging from evidence found in southern African cave paintings, and if we interpret the deeper meaning of the premise of narrative therapy, we may see how profound interpretations are and the impact of narratives themselves on our ways of life. For those familiar with Buddhist concepts, this will not be an out-of-the-ordinary interpretation of the world.

For my own part, experiences of mindfulness taught me that I was not my thoughts and also that the mind is a great storyteller; revealing how unreal some thoughts are, putting them into perspective, and helping me understand that the mind has the ability to be used not only to do things and interpret things but simply to be aware and that just sitting with something instead of interpreting it is at times a valid response. Mark Williams touches on what he terms "the doing mind" and the aware mind quite a lot in his writing (Mark Williams and Danny Penman,

Mindfulness: A Practical Guide to Finding Peace in a Chaotic World, 2011). As someone with psychosis, the storytelling attribute of my mind had the ability to overpower me at times in my life, and mindfulness gave me back my distance, control, and also enough awareness to observe and question thoughts. Often, psychosis is seen as something someone goes through, but for my own part I learned that it could be considered an exaggerated aspect of pre-existing characteristics essential to someone's nature...

Psychosis is a unique experience peculiar to each individual. For those not facing this, the following narrative could be seen as the best form of providing a basis for how this illness is embodied. In the autobiographical quote below, you will find my own version of this experience to clarify what I felt.

Excerpt from *Do You Have What It Takes?* — uncut edition by Jerome Sewell

> Years later the night sky was out and I remember warmth, [t]hen suddenly a penetrating feeling entered my heart like the whistle of a stream of wind shattering glass and my heart wept for what it had done to this man. The moments were heavy in the kitchen on that night. It was building up; my thoughts to return to my created spirituality and then shortly after my family moved home again and I found myself sleeping in the study at my grandmother's house. In the depths of the night after I had smoked weed and settled in my sofa bed, my favourite anime from childhood (Dragon ball Z) played. In a distorted perceptual experience, I heard the words echo into my soul 'The mystic art of ko ken', during an episode where the hero went to the afterlife to learn a Sacred art to defeat the greatest enemies he would face in his life, training in the heavens. And I would then go

to the heavens myself after an echoing inspiration told me to enter a period of meditation with the sacred arts I had received in my youth. I was called to enter a time of sacred learning in a time period mirroring Goku in the world of the kais; learning and raising my spiritual level to defeat the upcoming court case through elevating myself. The prayers came back, the incense came back and the native American chants came back. I sat and closed my eyes and the chants swept me away and deepened the intensity of feeling, then my body and mind were filled with light and fire. It feels real even now and I wonder how. Walking down the street after this I felt flames of pure bright yellow energy burning across my limbs and empowering me. My self-written mantras transformed my perceptual experience and the world felt like all that came in the future was meant to be and ordained; put in place for a response, destined like a tapestry that was already written. My mind was taken to skies of sweeping moments with yellow and bright light reaching across the earth.

From these moments I was carried into a period of revelation with constant inscriptions of prayers and meditations which took me deeper into this well, until I expressed all of my thoughts and dreams of what I would plan for the world; shaping a master plan for the building of my own civilisation whilst shaking the earth with my inventions and ideas (like a City of light built out of many ideas [I] received over years from spirituality and philosophy taught to me in my youth).

Alongside the narrative above, the assembling of the mind crowded with thoughts and feelings contains a medley of experiences. Poetry, we found again, can help to interweave this idea of thoughts, emotions, and sensory experiences. Below, the poems depict a vivid depiction of psychotic experience.

Reality
by Jerome Sewell

To be or not to be,
Is that not the question?
Truth, what is truth?
Down into mental planes,
It grows like moss from a swamp,
Crawling over his mind,
Symbols and meaning,
Experience and explanation,
Holograms of a real feeling,
Light sweeps him across the universe,
Arms and legs on fire,
Burning with each step,
Before friends became enemies,
Fate unfolds,
The tapestry of life,
All is meant and was meant to be,
Living tales of plots, vengeance,
demon kings,
Deeper and deeper,
The water streams downward,
Losing himself in incense,
Lost in possession,
To be or not to be,
that is the question,
Transfigured forms strike a mind,
Footsteps
cause thunder under lightning,
falling from the sky.

The odyssey to the underworld,
Finding meaning,

Seeking legends in a life of this world,
Over and over,
pages unfold,
Memories wrapped in presence that illuminates,
Is this a part of me?
Or something I found in my destiny?
Growing seeds of a possessed soul,
Red faces falling to the ground,
Visions of angels
on chariots of fire,
Signs and wonders,
Transmission to many doors,
Of a great many realities.

Returning to my breath,
It feels as firm as this water in front of me,
What will your mind see?
Is there a reality?
The atman,
The Brahmin says,
As he pressed record,
Souls,
Unfolding for the lessons of this life,
He told himself 100 times,
Even if returning to earth in 1000 lives,
The weight is enough,
The saint scribes,
A pen in a holy city,
Lit with grand mosques and colossal heights,
The word has a weight,
Transfigured, creating meaning,
The epoch of ancient bushmen,
The origin of thought,
Only found in the land of the blacks,

The blessed land,
Conceived by the heart,
Realised by the word,
As Nubian steps,
ground temples in Memphis,
Charcoal feet,
Hammer, steel and fire,
Shaping symbols,
As solid as his breath.

It is what it is,
I am what I am,
I am not my thoughts,
But it feels so real,
Until silence unknots,
Gautama awakens,
Under palm-strung trees,
Carnal gods throw spears,
Returning to my breath,
The mind,
My mind is the greatest storyteller,
Falling into past,
Tumbling into futures,
Shaping visions,
illuminating a realist feeling,
I am not my thoughts,
It is what it is,
I am where I am,
The child falls into a world of gods,
Falling head first through paper,
On other worlds,
mysteries in new spaces,
lightships through space,
His thoughts race,

Race, into clouds in Egypt,
Race into 100 worlds,
The master holds him softly,
A cage is broken by a soaring mind,
It is what it is,
I am what I am.
The storyteller,
Found the garden temple,
The great epoch,
Questioning ancients on mountains,
Questioning his own flicker,
To be still,
It is what it is,
I am what I am,
What is the question?
Out of this tunnel,
finding small light,
Out of my mind,
Finding what is,
Real but held,
I will hold my space,
I am not my thoughts,
Truth, what is truth?
What is meaning?
Shaped under sacred swords,
Soft and curious,
Distant yet luminescent,
To be or not to be,
That is the question,
Beyond existence,
It is what it is,
I am what I am,
The great revealing,
The great becoming.

ALTERNATE ILLUSIONS (A.I.)
by Mase Okor

What's real doesn't feel real anymore.

Close friends turn into distant strangers.

Authenticity seems to be a long-lost concept as the world is filled with fraudulent dangers.

Trust is a game of Russian roulette.

In a world full of artificial images, voices and people — who can we really trust?

Avoidance and attachment don't mix well in this intoxicating hell called heartbreak. I despise you and all the despair you caused me, I hate you so much, I hate myself too.

Having homed in on a very complex experience, consistent emphasis is placed on the role of mental perception. To conclude this chapter we speak about medical frameworks, methods of assisting changes in perceptual experience, and the role of services within this dichotomy as outlined below.

Perspectives of Recovery in Practice

Lurasidone, aripiprazole... there are many medications and many labels for a huge variety of created substances that regulate the activity of the mind. When one is in hospital, from my experience and the experience of others I know, medication is almost given sacred status as the great cure for mental illness. When working with forensic mental health patients, the level of impact that medication has on someone's assessed risk is arguably greater than the impact it has on those in non-forensic services, as it is often linked to someone's propensity to cause harm to others. I have a business partner who committed manslaughter after hearing a thought that took control of him during a fight. If mental health instability is seen to be the cause of violence, then there is a very direct correlation between the use of medication and propensity to violence in the view of some medical professionals. This then impacts service users' paths, such as with the use of community treatment orders, which ensure that someone who doesn't take their medication is sectioned and put back in hospital. This is despite the fact that according to the Royal College of Psychiatrists 30 percent of those with a condition will not relapse after not taking medication. The causes of psychosis are unclear, but it is largely believed to be caused by an imbalance of dopamine and serotonin in the brain; therefore in this sense psychosis has a biological underpinning which medication seeks to rectify. But neurological pathways and brain development are complex, and perceptual experience (which is directly related to psychosis) may be linked to neurological conditions but also to external factors through sensory experiences. In fact, what a thought is exactly is a deeply contested subject. Whilst medication causes neurological changes, does it always cause perceptual change? Which is arguably more complex. Once, when I was speaking to a responsible clinician, he stated to me that 30 percent of patients in his experience will not recover from their mental health symptoms, whilst a psychologist I worked with explained that there is a difference between witnessing a hallucination and how someone responds to their hallucinations. There are methods some people use to control their responses to these things.

I would encourage practitioners to now look more widely than medication in terms of what impacts perceptual experience. And there does indeed need to be more study into perceptual experience itself in relation to psychosis. What comprises a person's thoughts and responses to their thoughts? Often, imbalances are not the root cause, I would argue, and someone's emotional health, external factors, and a range of intangible parts of the personality such as perspective, beliefs, and other things may have a more profound impact or influence on mental stability and instability. Medication is one tool for one aspect of someone's mind but not necessarily the solution (high relapse rates for those with psychosis may be demonstrating this). For my own part, medication did not entirely stop elements of my psychotic experiences, but mindfulness did. A large part of my need came down to being able to observe, control responses to, and understand my thoughts. Practitioners can learn from this, I would argue, in that trying to constantly fix something, rather than accepting or simply assisting someone's responses to what is there for them at that time, may not always be the most appropriate thing to do. Practices that encourage reflection, inquiry, and observation whilst maintaining safety are important. The thing I disliked most about psychology sessions in hospital was that I was always asked reflective questions but not given the methods to change the issues identified, and I needed to find my own methods in the end (which actually led to me seeking out mindfulness). Mindfulness encourages acceptance and using our own aptitude when recognizing our problems, helping us to then find our own solutions. Encouraging service users to see the world through their own lens and accept their perspectives rather than challenging them, whilst working within this perspective (including their own experiences) in ways that progress towards goals based on their own value systems, is a good place to start perhaps. This can include encouraging the use of a person's own skills. When I was in hospital, occupational therapists and I had this relationship; where I came to them with my own goals and they empowered and mobilized this. For example, as a filmmaker my occupational therapists helped to get my laptop brought into the hospital so I could edit some of my own footage.

Mindfulness, I should note, is also demonstrating (through neurological studies) that we not only need to refine our understanding of what can change perceptual experiences but also understand how our brains change. The tools used in mindful practice to change both brain and perceptual activity, which can include awareness, gentle approaches to thoughts, curiosity, acceptance, and self-kindness, may provide pathways for allowing healing beyond the use of medication and provide new paths to long-term change.

Journey to the Underworld

We have now reached a stage where our journey, having taken us through early childhood, adolescence, adulthood offending, and psychosis, now brings us to the living conditions and dimension of experiences among those who are incarcerated, as an attempt to bring readers closer to understanding this whilst not having lived it.

Everyone's experience of the system is different. The experience of a prison or hospital is as variable as the sentences someone can get, the staff and cellmates they encounter, and so on. In a life-story account of a service user, called *Once Upon a Time in Brixton,* by Kray Matt, the gentleman recounted a whole list of people who died in the system (often through suicide). In my own experiences, I encountered some things I never knew of, such as self-harming and other things. Speaking to a young man in his early twenties from Wandsworth who entered prison, he described the place as giving him time to think. Another young man, also in his early twenties, who had spent a few years inside, told me he consistently used the time to read and get deeper into knowledge. These places (prisons and hospitals) are a paradox; they attempt to create opportunities and a regime that enables life development (for example the education and work systems in prison, or therapy spaces in hospital), but the very nature of the living conditions that people are put under makes the desired change and progress of people impossible at times — having a toilet in the same room as the man next to you, drug use, fights in exercise yards, being trapped behind a metal door and left alone by yourself. I was speaking to a man in my supported accommodation in 2020 and he was recounting to me how his time in prison was spent meditating, which resonated with me. For those with psychosis, prison may become a very different experience due to sometimes warped interpretations informing your experience.

A co-worker of mine once spoke about seeing into the future in regard to who was going to end up going back inside when he was in prison; he described those dedicated to pursuing prison work activities and those who had children being clearly dedicated to not returning. He spent five years inside and was heavily involved in the gang world in South London. For me, my experience over 18 months in prison was full of strange and twisted stories. Healing and repairing is the premise of mindfulness for some; finding grounding and stillness through your breath (which is always available to you) and not looking outside for stability but within. Being at peace with what is there for you in the moment, calming your threat system and nerves, and undoing at times the impact of trauma on your being...

Bringing this to the forefront of our understanding of someone's life necessitates us hearing directly what the sights, sounds and experiences are of people who have lived this. Whilst it is true that the above provides various encounters with this part of life, my personal account below of my own experience we hope goes some way to explaining what is lived by those going through this.

Excerpt from *Do You Have What It Takes?* — uncut edition by Jerome Sewell

In the blackened space of the induction wing I remember all of us as new members of the prison community standing together, being led and inducted into the space. They scanned my clothes and everything was taken from me on that day. I finally found myself in a cell with a young white man. My time at Wandsworth

Prison began with me going even further into the mentally constructed story and many visions and hallucinations started to shape; with me meeting spiritual guides, connecting with ancient ancestors and continuing to undergo the spiritual battle that now drew on and bore relations to what I was experiencing in prison (continuing the theme of experiences in the real world being distorted by a combination of mental interpretations and now false depictions made to seem like reality). I persisted, living in those two worlds of reality and my spiritual story which now [saw] me seek to elevate through meditation, prayers and training; setting my body on fire again throughout the space as I went deeper into aspirations to lift myself spiritually and physically amidst the conditions in my cell. In those days I was encountering spiritual teachers from my past and having DNA based ancestral visions; connecting to the djinn from my father's lineage. As this happened I formed a good relationship with my cell mate and we spoke about our crimes, life and views, smoked together and I recollect thinking of him as a masonic agent sent to tempt me when he spoke of aliens and the like. But in a thought closer to truth, I remember my regrets of not taking the European hostel trip around 10 cities offered by my university where I could have seen [starry] nights in Germany and Amsterdam. The incense smoked around the cell, the meditations were deeper and I was in the exercise field training for the early part of my stay in prison.

Having now gone through descriptive accounts, we are brought to poetry elements to convey what remains unsaid. Experiencing something, and your thoughts whilst experiencing what you are going through, are the features of the next poems.

Through Hell's Gates
by Jerome Sewell

On the passage to the underworld,
It is funny what a soul will find,
As funny as what the boy found in the peaks of a mountain,
Encounters and souls,
Descending,
Down to burly dungeons,
Forced in escape,
Dimensions, in different planes,
By the wayside of sights and sounds,
Mental doors,
Landings of a war zone,
For I travelled to hades,
Cast down by my being,
Where is the light?
They came in,
He fell down,
Unconscious,
Arms cut,
Wounds stripe his cellmate's countenance,
Lost in a senseless chaos,
The mound builds,
As I tumble further and further into depths,
Who will ferry me?
Behind doors with those who take life,
Those whose hearts accelerate,
Speeding from stolen cars,
The boy has become a man,
This place burns as hell's grounds,
A voice of flames,

My passage to the underworld,
Sinking,
Nights come out,
Strange voices came out,
Sirens within chambers,
Battlegrounds of beating,
They race now,
Containing monsters.

Waters fall next to thieves,
No worth, no privacy,
Urine mist stains this habitation,
Stories of evil,
A cover of thick mist over this landing,
Marching through fire,
The boy has become a man now,
Enlightened light has its own sound,
Awakened behind the dragon's gate,
This maiden behind walls,
Watches over him,
Healing,
Cultivating broken glass of a lost mind,
Will he survive?
Fire rises,
covering his chest,
That night when cannons sent jets,
soaking him,
alone in a holding cell,
Blistering cold,
holding him on,
The boy is a man now,
We have survived storms now,

So says the maiden trapped in walls,
Dig deeper,
Go further.

He holds his mindful breath,
Acceptance,
The old lion asked 'Do you accept it?'
Reborn now, reformed now,
My journey to the underworld,
Finding light in a room,
For there is nothing wrong here,
Depths of black space,
Reaching into nirvana,
Thoughts flicker,
unmoved stones in this garden,
I will not move,
Darkness,
as deep as an endless ocean,
Mending,
Within ceasing passages of time,
I can feel it stitching,
One with this mending,
The becoming,
Emerging in light,
As the lotus
emerges from chaos,
From earth's core,
To stars mapped in heaven,
I stood the test,
The becoming.
Tumbling from beneath earth,
The soil opens,
Unveiling day's light,

Emerging in mindful breath.
Silence heals all things.

One of Those Nights
by service users from the Bethlem Royal Hospital

The brain is mourning?!
And no matter how hard you try!?
The brain wants to speak,
have its 'voice' heard.
It won't be ignored!
No matter how hard one tries?
Reminiscence, recounting and recalling
the "life" led prior?
'One of those nights'…
Where there is nowhere else to look?
No place to feel any consolidation,
Nights that one must face only themselves.
Filled with judgment, beratement and self-loathing
Guilty… Sentenced… Imprisoned.
Surrounded within incarceration.
Enveloped in 'time'
Time, past by,
Behind and now gone!
Yet all time up ahead.
Set out, accounted for… Time to be served.
Entombed and now encased in consequence.
All are affected.
Inside the sum total of life's transgressions.
From the past, from behind, all echoes through.
Resonates, vibrates onto the daily existence.
Nobody can forget?
Forget why we are all here individually?

Locked in the truth of each own reality?!...
Maximum security prison!
Oppressively depressive
Volatile, vicious, degrading.
Subhuman incurring.
No less than I deserve.

I watch a younger 'me',
from a different space in time walk towards the window.
Stepping up onto the heating pipes, underneath the open window.
With its bars on the outside
Allowing a more open 'window'
With deep sorrow I brace myself for him,
I feel great pity and monumental love for this lonesome lad.
Head in hands I hear his thoughts as though they are inside me
Resonating... vibrating and calling out to an unknown future?
"Twenty-two years life"
The judge's words, all is a blur up to those words
That sentence,
It was not until this night
that I could begin to cogitate, to fathom the number?

Into the Frying Pan of a Psychiatric Hospital

Just as with the chapter focused on psychosis, this chapter occupies a unique place among the community of ex-offenders. In that even among those who find themselves in prison, a smaller section find themselves in a psychiatric hospital. In the account below we dig deeper into living conditions, particularly the trauma that can be induced by living in such environments themselves.

Despite the fact that both places hold people with criminal records, there is a vast difference between a forensic psychiatric hospital and a prison, but what remains common is the trauma of institutionalization. In 2021 I was working with a professor at King's College London running a research project on this subject and she interviewed a number of former patients in qualitative interviews, one of which I took part in. The reason this study was so pertinent was that whilst there is increasing acknowledgment of the trauma caused by life experiences, the trauma caused by institutions that are meant to help people in this situation is hardly ever acknowledged. In an HC20 report (a type of comprehensive assessment used in psychiatry), I read what was deemed to be my protective factors. This report stated that being inside a hospital with services was a protective factor, and I must say this is a gross misrepresentation of the truth of not just my experiences but those of many others, in my opinion. In my work with the Royal College of Psychiatrists I spoke during a meeting about the devastating impact that restraining procedures had on me in 2022, and instantly the meeting, full of other service user representatives (around seven in total) of all ethnicities and genders, chimed in with their own experiences of the same type of treatment during their admissions. During my time at the Bethlem Royal Hospital in 2019, I worked to create a group, called News and Views, which I created with another service user to give my peers a free space to discuss their problems and vent. During one of our first meetings, we spoke of the treatment that service users faced when being restrained, and many shared their experiences of this. For many others, as demonstrated by my meeting with the Royal College mentioned previously, such experiences have long-term damaging impact. Ultimately, people who have experienced this have been subjected to state violence. The depths of my trauma ran deep in hospital. For myself, mindfulness and its mantra about loving myself, alongside its ethos of not fighting feelings and thoughts and not responding in reactionary ways, quelled many of the traumatic responses caused not only by my own life but also by the system itself…

Below, my account of what traumatized me whilst under section provides an understanding of what people may face, as well as the subsequent poems.

Excerpt from *Do You Have What It Takes?* by Jerome Sewell

> In the [multidisciplinary] meetings known as a ward round, the power dynamic is shown in its most dramatic form. "The doctor is almost like God in here", was what Wayne said to me one day as we spoke in the garden. "They asked why everything is a fight or confrontation" Glen said to me. Tuesday was gossip day on the ward; who got what leave and privileges? Who got told [off] for bad behaviour? What disagreements took place? "That bastard", the patient would think about the doctor when leaving. It was a special day; a Tuesday full of anger and happiness (like dogs jumping to the table for the scraps of its master).

That is how it can feel around that table with those men and women. We speak of the trauma of institutionalisation and you may think of people having seizures in the room next to you or fighting, but the biggest struggle for me was to constantly have to fight for what I believed was mine; I mean my very self-determination and choice to do as I wanted with my life. The clinician across the table will sit there and tell you that they do not recognise that they are acting under legal powers to restrain your movements and liberty and that they don't recognise that they hold the keys to reversing a section of the mental health act that is keeping you caged like an animal. 'section is modern day slavery', are the words of an anonymous patient (no doubt) who scribbled in black pen on a post just outside the [R]oyal Bethlem hospital grounds.

The Trauma of Institutionalisation
by Jerome Sewell

Thrown into a dark room,
stilled with the presence of the night,
my arms are strapped behind my back,
they surround me, needles plunged down,
A rampage of chained ghosts erupt,
trapped in my chest,
tearing through my insides,
I can no longer contain the weeping of my thoughts,
tears and torment of loved ones scar my sheets,
They say that the sacrifice of the Lord is a broken heart,
and my soul has been smashed.
Clinging for strength,
I grab my pen,
footsteps pass,
window flaps open,

they stare at me,
witnessing the moments I first used my pen to cry,
taking solace in weeping ink.
As my destiny is decided by men in suits and women behind tables,
I fight to keep hold of who I truly am,
or become lost in the ignorance of a world that lacks understanding.
The wound was chained once more,
for the truth shall set you free.

The Trauma of Institutionalisation by Jason Harris

Waking up in cold sweats dreaming I'm back behind bars.
Wonder how to address all these mental scars.
Replaying the scenes in my head then feeling on edge
The anxiety of awaiting trial then actually being sent.

Cautious of my surroundings, constantly watching my back
The rattling of the keys the opening of the flaps
The uncomfortable feeling of sleeping on a mat.
Wanting to escape but knowing that I'm trapped.

Bars on the window, barbed wire on the fence.
Looking at a calendar feeling like there's no end.
Questioning everyone's motives if it's genuine or pretence.
Although this happened a while back it still seems quite fresh

A certain song, a tv show or even a scent.
Other times it might be linked to something someone said.
For some reason it causes the emotions and feeling to resurface again.
There are even some foods that tend to have the same effect.

TRAPPED IN THE REFRAIN
by Mase Okor

I'm sick of it.

I'm sick of me.

I'm sick of feeling like this.

Depression creates repression which permeates into suppression.

The ailments they spew onto me infest my psyche, heart and body.

My autonomy no longer autonomous.

Organs aching.

Heart breaking.

Words shaking.

The sickly fluorescent light burns my eyes.

The machines beep and keep shrieking putting me into a disorienting trance.

Blue sharp curtains begin to blur. Day in, day out.

My heart screams it shouts.

I lay in unceasing pain.

Sometimes it decreases but it comes back again.

Now and then.

It's a chronic, ironic, sardonic joke.

I never pictured my life like this.

If ignorance is bliss, actuality is a pain that persists.

Non-Violence and Rehabilitation

Now, having taken a long walk through the variety of life circumstances people encounter at the sharp end of society, we are brought to the part of emergence from this period of crisis, marking the turning point in a person's life. We must be true to the fact that not all of those who walk this path will reach this destination, but in our dedication to analyzing the causes of these conditions we find a clear necessity in learning the lessons of those who reform. The following chapters are dedicated to this side of the journey. The first step covered below regards criminal rehabilitation, particularly rehabilitation related to violence.

After listening to my interview with King's College London in 2021, my uncle wrote to me and said the kind of insight I had gained later on in life was something that could only come with age and experience. What he was mostly referring to in this instance was that insight I gained into accepting myself and being at peace with myself. Working with young men and women over the years, I have seen this issue time and time again; people being something they are not or being forced to become something other than themselves by acting "tough." In passing conversations, young men I work with have told me with bravado about how they could not be touched, or others our mentors have worked with have been affected by a façade of strength projected onto people around them. One young man sent to a young offenders' institution came out, and our mentor's assessment was that as this young man was the leader of his group, it created an air of strength. We call this the "circle of association" in our company and positive peer groups. When reflecting on his life, one of my colleagues who was heavily entrenched in organized crime acknowledged having no positive peer groups around him growing up.

The practice of being kind to oneself, avoiding the inner critic, and having self-compassion reminds me of many of the lives I have encountered. I had a conversation with a young lady from my neighborhood who reached out for mentoring support, and she described a deep feeling of isolation whilst commenting on the weight of another person showing her no compassion in regard to hardships, and she spoke of a sense of being asked to "suck it up." Another young lady I worked with in 2024 designed an entire workshop on women's mental health, mostly focused on what she referred to as the "strong black woman" stereotype. Her concept was based entirely on the idea that black women are pressured into being resilient when it comes to every challenge that comes their way and forced to be tough throughout their whole life. She based this on her own experience and a range of statistics.

In Mark Williams' inner-critic theory, mindfulness encourages us to have respect and kindness for ourselves rather than fighting and pushing ourselves. In an interview I held with a world champion of kickboxing in my youth, I was told that you should condition your body and suffer to prepare yourself, and this echoes a great many common sayings such as "Man up" and the hardening effect on people. This is whilst denying them the ability to be, feel what is there for them, and accept themselves. In Dialectical Behavioral Therapy there is the concept of learning to love your emotions rather than fight them. Mindfulness gave me back my self-respect…

You will see below some aspect of my own resolution in terms of criminal rehabilitation, focusing on what needed to be overcome.

Excerpt from *Do You Have What It Takes?* by Jerome Sewell

> *'Jerome claims that his index offence was a sociological phenomenon and said he grew up in a violent environment'*, wrote the clinical team whilst I was in hospital; they denied and dismissed

what was back then the true voice of a young man from south London whose world was completely removed from the middle class, picturesque lives of the clinical team (who know nothing of the time I lived in as a teenager) and who therefore refused to believe that the experiences of some of us are truly this grim on the streets of London. I did not grow up in poverty but truly I say with no pride that I am from a known hood in south London, where stabbings, robberies and shootings took place. *"But there's still what the rest [of society] thinks"*, the doctor who knew nothing of the streets, protested to me; as though the perception of wider society to the oppressed black community of south London meant anything in our dichotomy of life.

"The fact is when I was growing up as a [teenager] from the age of about 14, I grew up in what according to Scotland [Y]ard's records was the beginning of the escalation of gang and knife crime in the UK. Knife statistics rose and the numbers of young offenders perpetrating offences actually rose. I grew up in the midst of this and this was particularly when gang crime began to rise in London and I grew up in south London. Now in my area, there were a number of pretty big gangs and all you have to do is google them to find out what happened to their leaders; in the end some of them had to be deported to their home countries (such was the level of violence or threat they represented to the public). Growing up in [this] area I faced [a lot] of victimisation, I never ever joined a gang neither when I was younger nor when I was older but I was heavily [a]ffected by what they did to me and around me.... I was a young person that felt at imminent threat for my life and I'll give you the reasons why: a gang was after me and they were after me because I would read, I was a soft kid and I wasn't very naturally aggressive. I was just a very placid person and they picked up on that and they found out they could make a victim of crime out of me. These boys were recruited into the gang by elders in the years

above us in the schools. In the years above us, the members of that gang committed a murder in my local area and the murder itself has been dramatized by the BBC in a film about a young lady who lures a boy from Peckham into my local area and they set him up and kill him; they stab him to death. These are the elders by the way of the gang that is after me; they have killed someone and it has been dramatized. So I sat there and thought my life is probably in danger". ***(Jerome, workshop with [King's] College university, February 2021).***

In the end I chose peace and my true self, I chose my human placidness and fear of fighting over my demonic powers; such is the struggle of life over death. My soul is at rest now, for I am truly who I was meant to always be. *'I am the mind standing aloof without the falsity of the world'* ***(Poem by Grandmaster Gedo Chang).*** Somewhere in what I have written to all of you [you] may see that I have seen the will of heaven. I wrote once that one day I would perhaps be a pious Muslim; well then perhaps I will live to truly become a saint of the sword.

When covering this stage of a journey, just as with perceptual experience we have found it best covered in the vivid expression poetry allows for. In the poem below, you will find another account of how transitions towards sustainable lifestyles happen inwardly. It is important to note in this respect that in my own case meditation and Zen philosophy cultivated my change in thought processes which runs throughout as a theme in the piece below.

Love Yourself
by Jerome Sewell

The mirror looks at him,
They said,
If you stare into the abyss,

The abyss will stare back at you,
Walking,
On days sparkling yellow,
Sunlight shining across planes,
This hospital,
Moments before our sun sets,
Walking was his release;
A personal passage of reflection,
free with his own thoughts,
Hiking,
This child scaling hills,
Reaching that city on an island,
Crystal Palace,
This private resort,
Above poverty-stricken origins,
Through passages,
seedy roads,
Memories and meditations,
Appearing as holograms,
Shaded by the realist feeling,
Residing in another world,
Shaped from another dimension.

Visions interlock strides,
Passing shops and houses,
Flats and estates.
Firmly grounded steps,
Scenes move,
Conveying moments,
Fights, violence,
A record of choices,
Amidst deep decisions,
Directing trajectory,
In this strange part of earth,

I walk again,
As patient,
Weeks of mindful transfiguration,
Into awakened realisation:
Hug yourself,
For you are good enough,
My pen cries,
But my mind stills.

From then to now,
So the street prophet says,
What goes up
must go down,
Shaking,
Lowly to a mind's eye,
But with thoughts in high heaven,
What is weakness?
What is not good enough?
So what is pain?
The corridor passes him,
Footsteps travel, through shaking lenses,
Panic and heartbeats take his steps,
Spiralling to find peace,
And then what is weakness?
How will he draw strength?
Blinded by a world that worships hatred.

So desperate,
To be what he is not,
The punch swings,
The brick is picked up,
Helpless,
So what is strength?
The first stage of mindfulness

is acceptance,
Now he will be who he is,
He will lose himself,
He will lose his thoughts,
I am happy,
For I am me,
The shackles of what made me,
Falling to wind,
They won the battle, but will God win the war?
Thoughts and ink to high heaven,
I am good enough,
Through torment and fire,
I am sound enough,
They shook me,
But they could never make me.

My steps are acceptance,
Walking, forward to thoughts,
Towards souls lost in worlds that they never were,
Mind stilled and arms folded,
I will not force,
I refuse to push,
Gently now,
Softly now,
Are men hard?
Or how lost,
in falsities and scars?
The first stage is acceptance,
I will not push,
Ease of pulls,
Transforming.

Thoughts ricochet across blackened space,
I will not confront,

nor will I fight,
The becoming,
I am peace,
I am not my thoughts,
Minds wander,
Pulling backwards, to dissipate time,
For I will not fight,
What is destiny?
What will he become?
Folds under suffering,
Victim and perpetrator,
My pen cries,
Lost under shadows of a world,
Lacking understanding and insight,
I will not fight,
I am what I am,
It is what it is,
There is nothing wrong here,
I am who I am here,
Transpiring into this beat,
The becoming,
Gentle to a touch of myself,
I love myself,
I am myself.
Freedom.

To end this chapter, it is important — following on from the themes of dealing with and encouraging a gentleness and acceptance for oneself — to emphasize the role of a practitioner in helping someone to build a healthy relationship with themselves. Whatever our interactions and encounters with our service users, we all play a role in helping to build healthy individuals. The following conclusion concerns our advice to practitioners in helping their service users with this.

Encouraging Self-Compassion in Practice

Self-compassion, self-love, and self-attacking thoughts. For those unfamiliar with psychological terms, on the surface these can sound like sound bites conveying a cozy sense of self-indulgence, but from a mindful perspective this is really about self-acceptance and redefining your attitude to yourself and others in this life. For those who work with people predisposed to or involved in violent behavior, the concepts of strength, feelings of inferiority, low self-esteem, and the need to protect one's personage will not be unfamiliar concepts. During conflict mediations that my colleagues have carried out, a recurring theme of feelings of disrespect is ever prevalent; for example, during a mediation exercise rival gangs taunted each other about a rival who had been stabbed, causing the meeting to break down. What is our function here as practitioners? How do we help someone to see themselves as above negative responses to a situation and reduce their feeling of a need to use force? In the same way, self-compassion teaches us to take time with ourselves, accept the negatives of ourselves and encourage growth, a mindful understanding which encourages us to handle our service users with respect, enough compassion and understanding, not judge them; and reinforcing a caring and positive belief in them as people is often enough to help to create a safe space where people feel free to be vulnerable. During the Tree of Life intervention I have mentioned, a service user stated that taking part in this intervention made him feel the most comfort he had felt during months of admission, and I would state this is because we gave him the space to be honest with his thoughts and feelings and safe enough to open up. In interventions that Therapeutic Productions has led, during film rehearsals we have had actors with autism call the space safe and a supportive environment, amidst a world they often feel misunderstood and unrecognized in. Even with my own colleagues, when they have inquired about my criminal history

I have discussed the victimization in my youth and they have responded by reinforcing that I should never feel judged by them. This is in much the same way that young men who have cried in front of me may have felt free to do so because they recognized I had a non-judgmental attitude and compassion for them. These conditions, if created by us as practitioners, will often lead to safe spaces for people to be free with themselves whilst we use an approach of supportive language that builds someone's esteem, true respect for their individual qualities and who they are as people (not simply as service users). This is added to by genuine care that can reinforce people's desire to be comfortable with themselves, accept themselves, and remove a hard exterior that may force them to be and act other than themselves.

Paths to Freedom

Following the emergence from violent ideation and thought processes covered in the last chapter, we have decided to provide an account relevant to those who practice mindfulness in regard to their further development, given that our work to a large extent concerns the impact of mindfulness, meditative practice and Zen philosophy regarding individuals who face these experiences. As a result, below we begin this by relating the subject of choice and free will as an element of controlling one's thoughts and actions and its further implications for those involved in mindful practice.

Choices, free will; these are age-old concepts with age-old debates. All the way back to the ancient Roman Empire and early Christendom, Origen of Alexandria in his works talks about the individuality of the soul and its gains and losses being a consequence of its free will (Origen, *The Complete Works of Origen*, AD 185–254). Fast forward to the European Enlightenment in Western civilization and John Locke, one of the founders of libertarianism and a father of modern liberalism, espouses the concept of the rights of man and every man having "the right within his own property," embedding the concept of liberty through a sense of freedom being an innate part of nature (John Locke, *Two Treatises of Government*, 1689). Whilst Jeremy Bentham, laying the foundations of legal philosophy, goes deep into an exploration of the concept of intention and causality in his works (Jeremy Bentham, *An Introduction to the Principles of Morals and Legislation*, 1789).

But this is by no means a solely Western conversation; in the past I have had conversations and interviewed heads of the Hindu Council in Great Britain who have defined the concept of the *atman* or soul in Hinduism and how our lives are determined by what our souls choose to experience whilst seeking *moksh* or liberation. The Quran emphasizes that the difference between the three types of creations — man, djinn, and angel — is that both djinn and man have free will whilst the angels do not; hence the reason why Satan in Islamic faith was a djinn possessing the will to disobey God in the first instance, which an angel cannot do (Holy Quran, chapter 7, verse 11).

In Buddhist teachings, the samurai concept of "doing for the doing" or "pure action" is discussed, whilst the will of heaven is described by some as an instinctual presence within us that possesses a knowing, and as such, true actions are often those that are only to be found in the moment in a state of awareness (Kemmyo Taira Sato, *D.T. Suzuki and the Question of War*, 2008). The Eightfold Path in Buddhism emphasizes this in terms of right action and right understanding.

This topic has been picked up by cognitive psychology which emphasizes automatic thought-processes and the autopilot modes that many find themselves living in, where consciousness of thought and action cease and we are no longer in control of our responses (Suma P. Chand, Daniel P. Kuckel, and Martin R. Huecker, *Cognitive Behavior Therapy*, 2023). Through five years of mindfulness practice and eight years of meditative training, I have discovered that the true benefit of awareness can only be experienced, in my view. As mindfulness finds a place in our medical system, it has been divorced from its Buddhist origins so that it becomes a secular practice. Truly there are many benefits to this that have made this practice very inclusive as a result; however, there are consequences. Zen meditation, which mindfulness meditation is derived from, stems itself from the Mahayana school of Buddhism, which emphasizes practical experience. There is now an academic dimension to mindfulness, and I have experienced at first hand psychologists teaching mindfulness without its practice, purely as an academic exercise, when unlocking its benefits can only come from first-hand experience, from what I understand. I would emphasize that this necessity of practical learning as a methodology by which the teachings of mindfulness reach the student is derived from Zen cultural methodology, which is experiential...

Following on from this approach of reducing the extent of the use of automatic thought-processes, the excerpt below deepens the personal impact this can have, not only on the individual but on their life going forward.

Excerpt from article "The Art of Occupation: Wielding the Mind," published by *OTNews* by Jerome Sewell

> With regards to mindfulness, this practice allowed Jerome to control his thoughts and relieve stress, and to stay in a balanced emotional state. 'When I finished my first session of mindfulness, my mind felt so free it was unbelievable,' he remembers.
>
> 'It allows quality time to be given to yourself and deep relaxation and concentration to take place. When life's burdens become too intense, it allows you to free yourself — an essential skill in building up your own threshold in dealing with stress and intense thoughts.'
>
> Ron Maddox, the mindfulness instructor at the Royal Bethlem Hospital, and member of the Chaplaincy team, says of the practical benefits of mindfulness: '[The aim is] to loosen up (to put ourselves at ease), to overcome rigidity in our thinking, in our habitual attitudes, rituals, obsessions, and to open up the way.
>
> 'We are free to take the next step to the inner freedom that was always ours, and to step away from fear, distress, anxiety, the past or whatever else it may be that restrains and limits us.'

A key theme that is consistently highlighted in this side of our discourse is the notion of change, not a fleeting change but sustainable emergence out of a lifetime of negative patterns. When exploring this issue, often it can come down to the practice of observing and acting in the moment, and the poem below is designed to explore this active power of what this observance can bring to someone's thought processes and actions.

Liberty Wind
by Jerome Sewell

The atman,
So what is moksh?
Choices define reality,
Brahmins decree,
So the lens closes in,
In confines where time ceases,
Spiralling passages of time,
Lord Shiva telling fables of a seed,
Into actions,
further into futures,
As the cub claws through forests,
Branches of trees hang down,
Amidst thick smells,
clouding air,
He falls,
he rises,
He is struck,
Still, still I rise,
If I had returned for 100 lives,
Over the passage of thousands of years,
One lesson is worth redemption,
Returning to the breath,

That rising chest,
Which opens a new world,
Of freedom futures,
Of choices as free as wind,
Smoke opening him,
Swelling a release.

Life force,
The Undoing,
The becoming,
Choices,
Freedom in steps,
Caught in the living,
Free from the walking dead,
Liberation,
in the becoming,
Abstract and undecided,
Only to be conceived by the heart,
Realised by the word,
Returning to breath,
An officer standing,
At ease,
At attention,
Ready to walk through doors,
The bodhi under a palm tree,
When we sit, we know we are sitting,
When we eat, we know we are eating,
Presence,
What a choice,
Unheld by automation,
The becoming.

Breathe
by Jason Harris

Can you imagine feeling like you're unable to breathe?
Holding on to a small glimmer of light that I could barely see.
Hearing voices with no faces, conversations about me
Making threats towards my loved ones but hiding behind the scenes.

The darkness had almost consumed, and stigma made it feel bleak.
Drained from hypervigilance carefully scanning the streets.
Not knowing who to trust or who to believe.
A bit like the movie *Quiet Place* desperately wanting to speak.

Questioning my past and wondering who they could possibly be.
Feeling burnt out but too afraid to fall asleep.
I'm at a point where I am so fed up and desperate for some peace.
I tried all that I could think of including old school remedies.

Put on medication but still there was no release.
That's when I turned to God and prayed for him to intervene.
Shortly after I noticed that my breaths began to increase.
The next thing I knew I was in front of a class trying to help others believe.

Slowly my perspective started changing and the tension started to relieve.
For a long time, I could actually see beyond what I was visually able to see.
It's been a while since I've been able to dream.
Each breath brought healing allowing my mind and body to feel free.

Breathe
by Mase Okor

Freedom lies inside the hearts of those who have courage.
Courage to dream, courage to be seen, courage to explore life beyond their means.
It is the remedy held in each repressed breath.
It is the leap of faith that comes after a thousand steps.

The suppressed soul suffers more than those who live openly.
Uncover the restrained feelings you claw shut in your rib cage.
Fly.
Soar.
Sing.

Let your lungs free.
Be who you need to be.
You are all the freedom you'll ever need,
Breathe.

The last element of this chapter, having explored this theme of mindful change, takes us down a different stream of thought. Whilst we may not feel that existential questions of life become relevant in our work practice, to bring this matter to a conclusion we seek to gently widen the scope of the implications of our engagement with service users and look into far more difficult questions than measurements of success and actually how our perspectives as practitioners on life itself provide an effect on how we deliver our services.

Redefining Reality in Practice

What is our past? What is our future? In mindful practice we deepen our awareness of reality, and in the course of this, thoughts are distinguished from direct, imminent experience. I work with a professor at a university, and once when we were talking about a research project that we were going into, he spoke about understanding that people's actions and people's thoughts about their own actions are two different things; emphasizing the difference between perceptual experience and reality. The practice of sitting and noticing what our present thoughts and feelings are (although perceptual in part) may represent our only true encounter with external reality; separate from our perceptual experiences that stand by themselves. When you are sitting by the bank of a river, the wind blowing on your skin may evoke feelings and sensations that are experienced through the lens of perception, but they are a perceptual encounter based upon something that is external to you and does indeed exist at that point in time; making this moment of awareness starkly different from our thoughts about what may happen at work the day after or what happened at our home yesterday (which could be regarded as almost entirely mental constructs at that moment). The "now" is a powerful acceptance of the way things are, and even a momentary awareness of the now inspires a sense of acceptance; the mindful state of awareness itself, I would argue, dissipates illusory experiences, contextualizing and bringing perhaps one of the few forms of truth grounded in existence. Not as we interpret it but as our mind and body directly experiences it, aligning sensory experience and perceptual experience; joining the thought with that part of us that occupies the continuum of space and time we exist in. It is said in mindfulness therapy that the body knows how we feel before the mind does; again, a sensory experience may be perceptual in part, but it leans on something from outside of our minds, something that is independent of our thoughts (which is what perhaps grounds us during breathing exercises). We are brought back from our mental space into a space that occupies a place in an external world.

As practitioners, it is the case that the decision-making of those we work with comprises a source of what interventions we use and how we intervene with them; whether it be a probation officer who puts in place license conditions that prohibit someone from drinking alcohol or a psychologist who writes recommendations for certain types of treatment. This decision-making capacity within someone, going back to previous chapters, is linked to our predictions and mental inventions as practitioners concerning what the service user will do and what paths they will take. But herein lies a problem with the premise itself: if we are to adopt a mindful understanding of decision-making, it may lead us to accept that decisions are momentary and in many ways independent of causality. This is difficult to accept in societies that for hundreds of years have subscribed to Newtonian concepts of cause and effect; it challenges the entire premise of what we know about how things take place in the world as a whole. In this sense, one thing does not lead to another; predictions based on purely theoretical underpinning are less relevant as a result. Mark Williams emphasizes this in his work by explaining that traditions of meditation represent the propensity to use the mind in a way modern societies are unfamiliar with, and I would extend this argument to state that mindful thinking encourages an unfamiliar outlook on how things take place in the world and come to be. From my practice, learning about this power of noticing a moment, I have found that controlling the passage of time itself that governs us and our actions has the ability to create spontaneous responses that open a new door of thought and action, to break the chain of events that creates seamlessness from one action to another, to break automatic thought-processes. The mindful curiosity taught by teachers emphasizes this by relying on awareness to notice things, investigate, and interpret purely by heightening your awareness enough to open the mind to previously unfelt and even unknown sensations, in the body for example. Ron Maddox emphasizes this in his article contribution in *OTNews* when he describes "opening up the way." Such is the power of the mindful breath.

Before leaving hospital, a service user in a violence-focused group that I attended spoke about ensuring that he pauses when he is angry; this allowed him to control his responses. Although this is common, we could recognize it as a mindful practice that encourages awareness and then allows for new choices. So for practitioners, who are encouraged to draw on a pile of notes during meetings concerning a person, it may be necessary to accept that even from one meeting to the next the service user's propensity for change is imminent and that decisions are as much dependent on inward factors not determined or influenced by external factors as they are by circumstance — even leading to the potential that a service user may transform their perspective or course of action instantly and without warning.

Again, if we step away from models of goal orientation and step towards one of cultivation, we may recognize that change is organic, inasmuch as the growth of a plant is a combination of factors affected by an individuality of circumstance concerning natural elements. In this form, we may become more aware of the fact that our intervention's success or determination of effectiveness is not based on our outcomes but on our intentions, and that unintended and unexpected consequences are a natural part of an intervention — that the goal of intervention is of less consequence than the way it is delivered, the nature of delivery and approach. Often, compassion is enough to ensure the impact of an intervention, even removed from other determinants of quality (such as monetary value or even duration of time spent) in some cases. Our job is to create a condition for growth that cannot be predicted by ourselves and cultivate compassionate intention for a person rather than goals and targets, and in the vein of this chapter, to encourage awareness, a noticing of the present, acceptance of what is there at this time for the service user, and a breathing reflective space that allows a growth of someone's thoughts to make truly informed decisions.

What the Future Held

To bring us to the end of our walk through the life of a person we work with and have worked with, it is time to conclude with our hope for the future, a hope that is only brought to life through examples, as we evidence in the success stories in the account below.

The American dream has come to epitomize a kind of material status that is accessible for those of us who will strive for it. Much of this dream is embodied in wealth, money, and luxury: nice houses, nice cars, and many other things that not only depict status but also symbolize the ideal lifestyle. In 2021, my company interviewed young people during a media production course, and one young lady from a sixth-form college in Croydon between 17 and 18 years of age spoke about wishing to have a five-bedroom house. My colleague (who was mentoring her) began to break down what the costs of her mortgage would be in that case, and she was told how much her chosen career path would need to give her financially. On that day, she was not the only one who spoke of this type of house as being their long-term goal. On the same course, I went on to work with another young lady from my local area, Thornton Heath, who was of the same age, and eventually she left my organization and went on to pursue studies and part-time work. One year later she came back to me and wrote a message saying that she wished to concentrate on her personal development and not just money anymore, and another man I worked with for two years told me that after entering full-time work he was unfulfilled and lacking purpose, despite having a higher income and financial comfort. These encounters interested me and related to what I have found in my own experience, in that in modern European countries and elsewhere we have found ourselves bound to a mainstream culture where artists in music videos drive high-value cars and there are entire programs dedicated to celebrity houses. According to some film experts, the directors of the film *Scarface*, a gangster motion picture, stated that their storyline of a young Cuban immigrant who becomes a gangster is a reflection of seeking the American dream. In my own experience, after having spent time away, I have met many gangsters and criminals who spoke of the amount of money they have made in their lives.

As evidenced by a number of tragic suicides among the rich and famous, all the way down to the experiences of the youth I work with, quality of life and peace of mind appear not to be dependent on money (or not entirely at the very least). And in my own time in this world, I also began by having dreams of wealth in my teenage years, but my life provided a much deeper value in the end...

Only an individual themselves can really explain their measurements of their own achievements and what they make of it. Important as it has been to provide accounts and analysis, we can see from the quote below what an individual will make of their own journey.

Excerpt from *Do You Have What It Takes?* – uncut edition by Jerome Sewell

And so it had come to pass, Allah ensured my destiny was fulfilled and likened to Geb, the God of Earth and first pharaoh of Egypt, who after receiving the mercy of divine power and grace, following his near destruction caused by the sin of his own heart, went on to become a just ruler and leader. I found that light in my past and used it as a rope to climb out of the deep pit I had fallen into. Only to emerge like a blue lotus out of chaos. Over the passage of time that does [not] exist [except] as a perceptual construct, every dream, covenant and mission that I had held in my life was fulfilled in the five years I had left hospital:

In April 2024 I was at the height of God's mercy over me and his majesty that shone the light of the sun over my future. At the age of 15, driven by the mission to build a business to reform the social economic structure of my community, I was now a managing director of two organisations 16 years later and over this time had reached the goal of raising over £100,000 for these companies, even exceeding this and raising over £500,000 over the past 5 years, (another goal I had set with Christian Douglas, all the way back when I was living in a hostel in 2020). This was whilst employing almost 300 people from all corners of the dispossessed and aiding the lives of hundreds more. The inspiration in hospital which told me that my purpose in life was to use film to spread moral messages had now been fulfilled, and after the decision made with Chris to form a department, I had now built not just that department but also another from its foundation to its heights (now gone national). Culminating in the creation of a feature film reaching tens of thousands of people, soon to go international and delivery of over 6 media courses inspired by my martial [arts] experiences, that had led to the creation of over 10 short documentaries with 55 youth. And now a second feature film was on the move and backed on a national level and again, even another film and also a documentary drama were pushing forward, blasting creative light.

And on a personal level, I had returned to Africa, stepped on the sacred soil of the blessed land; residing inside the palaces of my emperors and forefathers during pilgrimage. Lastly, I secured my own flat, freed myself from the system by ending my probation license, leaving mental health services and provided blessings for my loved ones over this time.

In 2021, I took my younger sister to visit a Zen Garden maintained by a Zen monk whose teachings where fundamental to my rehabilitation. When we travelled the Monk told us that one of the stones inside the garden had one part of it buried underneath the ground and stated that this stone was buried out of respect for the invisible component of human nature. Like the stone in this zen garden; buried underneath the soil that stands peacefully, it was the Zen and holy part of me that bore the cultivation of rain and soil that [saw] the tree of my fate become what it became. And over this time, the craft of writing became a self development tool and exertion of the power inside of me. I used to think the inscriptions were my light but at last I realised I was the light.

At my new height as an executive producer, project manager and managing director we had completed shooting half of my new film the Prodigal Monster, working with over 100 dispossessed people, delivering our interventions 10 times over, after raising over £60,000. As a new storm was carrying us, I steered this ship, where onboard [were] masterpiece artwork creations, many hit soundtracks and all other colours found within the collective creative power of film. Driven by my hospital admission and the need to bring my inspiration to those caught in the same trap.

In all things the heart will direct your path and in the past (as retold) my journey through martial [arts] training had led to zen inspired practice which reformed my soul. Leaving hospital my practice continued and brought peace and stability to my mind and life; I had become more attentive and found joy with peaceful moments;

> like times I would sit in a garden seeing the blossom of flowers whilst smoking a [H]amlet cigar.
>
> Later on, the same cigars were smoked in front of a river's moving tide in Kingston years later. It is true (as always), that there were at times pain, anger and strife but a silence had kept me grounded over time; holding me through my mindful breath. I gained a new teacher as I integrated fully into a community based, self-led care. I practised with him, his method was different from Ron [M]addox and I learnt of the mind and its nature through him. Upon his advice, I used a technical aid and began practicing daily in 2021. It has now been 5 years of practice and along that path I heightened my cultivation through reading and new forms of practice, found in an 8 week program in 2022, which is reminiscent of the cultivation of flowers. Much of life became zen after discharge; much quieter and much softer than the past.

But although my mind continued to expand, there are no blessings without works, and in truth it was also my new career that shaped my heart and mind (through compassionate service).

I must add in the final chapter that whilst being appreciative of the blessing that took place later on in my journey, this reflects one image of an ultimately fulfilling life, but I have met many people, both older and younger, who have overcome their turmoil and come out with great stories at the end, and much more of this needs to be shared. At points in this text, I have leaned on the account of Kray Matt in his autobiography, and as someone who I work with and am friends with, his journey truly strikes me as one of the greatest symbols of hope I have come across. This gentleman, who spent over 20 years inside the system, not only found his way out of an incredible darkness most could not imagine but also found his way to getting married and having children. These are the stories that we hope offer hope of lasting change. The authors I have written this piece with also have their own stories of lasting change, as Jason Harris explains:

> Since coming out of hospital there have been many positives. Looking back to how I was to now, I feel so much stronger. I feel like this experience was all part of a molding and shaping in lots of areas. The path I was on wasn't good for me: the smoking, drinking, partying all combined was taking its toll on me, like the saying "Everything happens for a reason," but whatever the reason it brought me closer to God which I am so grateful for. Before my experience I couldn't see myself being a published author or tutor; I hated being the center of attention even when playing football (I would just focus on the game). With the grace of God, I have gone from this shy guy to speaking at events and universities sharing my experiences and advocating on multiple platforms, facilitating groups for people with unusual experiences. I'm also in the process of writing my second book, *Through a Loving Lens*, a follow-up from my first book, *Retrieval of the Soul*, and to add to that this, this current project with Jerome Sewell and Mase Okor. I also work full-time for NSFT (Norfolk and Suffolk NHS Foundation Trust) Early Intervention in Psychosis team which is now approaching six years and am also involved in research and feel humbled by the transformation. God has been good and has also blessed me with a marriage and two kids. I hope people see this and feel encouraged in their own journey. My advice is not to give up and to keep the faith; I know not everyone shares the same belief, but Jesus is and has been my savior.

The third contributor to *The Burning Breath Chapters*, Mase Okor, shares an aspect of his journey that speaks to the inspirational achievements that new generations are accomplishing in their lives, bringing us into seeing hope for all of our futures:

> I would say one of my greatest artistic achievements would be publishing a poetry collection before 25, and selling over a hundred copies in four weeks. Also a personal achievement would be getting a first-class degree in Drama and English; it wasn't easy and it's something I am personally very proud of.

It is only fitting at this point, having articulated each chapter theme with poetic elements, that this final chapter uses the same medium in the poem below to capture the feelings of someone who has gotten to this place in their life.

Dreams Dog
by Jerome Sewell

To feel such peace,
Driven by need,
Self-love,
Self-service,
Have I fallen into a new life?
this therapeutic life?
He questioned,
Quality of being,
Picture feelings and sights of green serenity,
bathed in golden light,
I walk elevated,
As though on soft clouds,
In a sphere of existence on earth for many unfound,
It was said his desires led to his suffering,
Aside from dreams,
Visions of wealth,

Champagne lifestyles,
Skylines,
What will we find much deeper?
Within our make-up, inside our very structure,
That desire for peace of mind.
What a strange world this is;
In a lunatic asylum,
freedom taken,
But achieving this vital ending,
Many drink and inject their lives away seeking.

Dreams dog,
Chasing my dreams dog,
The rhymer rhymed,
What is worth?
I search for my wanting,
What is service?
In need of my calling,
The seed found itself under deep dust,
It has not questioned,
How tall shall I grow?
Will I reach the heavens?
The shell filled with life,
Sits as the bodhi under palm shades,
Consuming showers of crystal-clear drops,
The great light of an all-encompassing star,
Waiting to become what it was destined to,
Dreams dog,
They said they need jewels,
They claimed a need of gold,
In quest of, searching,
For that found in fading,
For the heavens pass a thousand worlds.

The child walks,
The man sits,
The elder listens,
On the long road,
Heading to extinction,
When great lights fold,
Still holding on,
The first stage is acceptance,
What are you seeking?
Where is your treasure?
Where are you entering?
Dreams dog,
What will you find?
On a passage without time,
Is this not enough?
Dreams dog,
Where is my peace dog?

Even if 1000 diamonds descended,
It could not replace my never ending,
The moment,
The first stage is acceptance,
So what is contentment?
Living on the long walk,
What I have found transcends planes,
Unmoved by storms and thunder, passing rain,
Impermanence in tapestries,
a constant earth-struck tale,
The now,
The river calls for stilling,
The becoming.
I am what I am,
It is what it is.
Freedom.

And having now analyzed and interpreted an ultimately successful example of journeys, we are brought in this final set of recommendations to practitioners below to what our own work-life contributions can be to these individuals and how best to help them reach this destination.

Lasting Rehabilitation in Practice

Lasting rehabilitation — that much desired impact that not only professionals but even government departments are seeking. In the end, this has become one of the ultimate determinants of the success of both interventions and institutions, an all-encompassing outcome. In monitoring and evaluation, I have recorded monthly reports on 40 young offenders over a six-month period; added to this I have a number of mentees who I have personally worked with over a two- or three-year period. What I have found by and large is that a solid pathway or occupation that allows someone to invest their time in things that progress their personal, social, or financial welfare, combined with an almost unshakeable decision to not return to a life that is no longer wanted, seems to be the primary thing that determines whether someone's rehabilitation is lasting. This is in combination with new social groups that do not provide temptation in regard to old habits. I think of one young man I have worked with for over three years now; when we first met he was battling an immigration case and was unable to work, therefore having access to almost no money after coming out of prison. When he was first referred to me, I remember him struggling to find the money to take the train, but from then onwards, every opportunity provided to him he took for his own development; essentially because he had decided to strive relentlessly (despite any obstacles) to advance his self and his goals. Fast forward three years later and he now is in full-time work, has his own place, and delivers presentations inside the Houses of Parliament. Amidst progress reports, I have found through media analysis that the majority of young people who did not reoffend over a six-month period were surrounded by a range of services that catered for their different needs (including housing, education, employment, and life support); at the same time as this, they had often left an old lifestyle behind them and, as referred to previously, through vocations most of the time they were taking part in something that provided a consistent pathway to advancing their life and facilitating a forward movement, which (as mentors put it) occupied their time.

I am surrounded by colleagues who are ex-offenders or previous users of psychiatric services and who have sustained their rehabilitation for 15 years plus, or 5 years plus, and having seen so many of their journeys, I can relate to them. I can remember talking to one colleague and both of us recognizing that often our journeys began with an intervention earlier on in our lives and then a series of life lessons, experiences and encounters later led us to gradually shed, piece by piece, aspects of our lives that were flawed. For my own part, there have been many aspects to what created my sustainable change: from my mother telling me upon discharge to not engage again with old negative friends, to my employment journey with Unique Talent, and to my encounter with my mentor Reginald Enqi at the age of 15, who inspired me to get involved in business; thereby laying out pro-social ambitions that gave me a positive focus for years to come. This was alongside other changes around my lifestyle that took place through hospitalization and mindful meditation. Like many forensic service users, there were many things I needed to shed: childhood trauma, psychosis, drug addiction, violent behavior, moral defects; and elements I needed to overcome, such as financial dependence, community supervision, and maintenance of mental stability upon discharge. These represent intersectional needs as well as disadvantage.

As professionals, how do we ensure that our interventions are truly contributing to this ultimate goal and how is it that we ensure lasting impact? Reflecting, I think we must realize that each stage of a service user's journey contributes negatively or positively to their ultimate path; in Unique Talent we often speak of sowing seeds for years to come that will grow. A person's journey, after all, is ultimately an accumulation of experiences, interventions, and encounters. I have worked with a number of young people who left my service and went to work as actors for the BBC, entered full-time work, or attended university, and I have come to realize that for many service users, my provision represents a middle ground for them to develop skills and grow until ready for the next stage of their journey. For professionals, simply providing the best provision that aids a service user for a point in time, thereby enabling them to reach the next stage successfully, is enough. However, longer-term provision or provisions that I would cite as having the most far-reaching impact are those that might be time bound but have such a profound impact that they reshape someone's world and perspective; giving them something they take with them for years to come. Once, I was speaking to a partner from Bettering Education in Croydon, and he spoke of his desire to create provisions of such a high quality that they provide what we might call a "wow factor" when young people take part in them, and this was based on his own life experiences: a number of school and college trips gave him such an inspiration that it caused long-term impact. I have spoken to young people who sometimes years after leaving my service will cite knowledge or experiences they have taken with them, and others I know have cited this about other services. Often, as regards provisions, whilst direct service delivery is important, it may be more intangible things (perhaps in the form of knowledge, advice, or impact) that change someone's perspective and may end up having a long-lasting effect. If these gains are combined with enough social integration for people's time to be occupied with positive things and progress towards their own goals, then it creates a path of consistent development.

As professionals, guiding our service users to these paths by opening doors for them can be helpful; however, we must be true to the fact that it is people's own motivations within themselves that will always truly open doors for them. When I was staying in supported accommodation, the staff asked me to attend a meeting with one of the heads of this provision, and after hearing my journey, he turned to me and emphasized that the things I spoke about were my achievements and that I was ultimately responsible for these things. This recognition was new to me, as there is a tendency to sometimes claim credit for what our service users accomplish. The reporting systems of funders don't help this by asking for direct correlations at times between interventions and things like criminal rehabilitation (which are not only rarely dependent on one factor but are ultimately down to the autonomy of the service user themselves).

Another thing that must be noted is persistence and stability. In a mindful sense, we could recognize this as the difference between engagement in exercises and practice. A practice, in this sense, differentiates itself by a consistency and regularity. From firsthand experience I have noted how consistent practice of mindfulness can help to maintain stability, but whilst I would recommend trying mindfulness to anyone, in truth any practice, occupation, or feature of someone's life which gives them emotional and mental balance, nourishment and contentment is important to the maintenance of that stability, grounding, and well-being needed to balance the mind; so that right decisions are made that do not undo changes. You could liken this to the need of a plant to receive consistent watering.

As a last thought on this, perhaps above all things when we speak about intangible skills, benefits and knowledge is that skill that we describe as "insight"; a term that medical professionals in particular will be aware of, referring to someone's knowledge of themselves and their own condition. All too often, there is an attempt to infer that insight merely represents a regurgitation of medical professionals' views by service users. Once, when in hospital, I said to a psychologist that I believed I might have to stay on medication for the rest of my life, and when I said this (if I'm being honest) it was a simple lie on my part. I said this because I knew that telling them this would work in my favor (so I played the game, so to speak) and then when my insight was reviewed, my comment was documented as evidence that my insight had increased (just as planned). This is a debasement, in my view, of what insight truly is and its potential for long-term change. True insight, I would state, is not agreement by a service user with the views of professionals; it pertains to a more intimate and deeper knowledge of oneself. My true insight only really came when I started mindful practice, and in my case, mindfulness equipped me with a much greater knowledge of myself and how my thoughts and feelings worked; alongside patterns of behavior. When true insight is gained, both in a recovery and criminal rehabilitation sense, it becomes an incredibly powerful skillset and provision of knowledge that has the propensity to cause deep change and even inward transformation in some. From a professional's point of view, the best option in this respect for cultivating this ability, in my opinion, is to begin to see life through the lens of a service user and be open to truly understanding their perspective and then have meaningful discussions where knowledge, advice, and analysis can be shared. Once, a longstanding mentee, when speaking to me about his fear of living in a violent environment, had these discussions with me in a way where we both spoke from the perspective of how things are commonly seen in street-wise communities. We spoke as members of the same community, simply with different perspectives, but the same understanding of common concepts and languages. Lastly, true insight comes from an inward development, and this development can come through different interventions and sources, but what is common with all of them is a space to share, to question, to understand. I mean by this to develop that curiosity talked of in mindfulness which comes from a place of safety, which allows new understanding and views to form. Every practitioner can have a role in this. I used to work with an occupational therapy technician in hospital who spoke to me about the nature of clinical services, and I learned a lot about growth and development from him. One of my colleagues in Unique Talent has changed my perspectives on many things over time. In both cases, this has happened despite this not being their function as professionals, simply by creating an open and progressive space, whilst being open to sharing views and discussions that allow people to talk in their own way and bounce off each other. Even family members such as my grandmother, mother, and uncles do this a lot with me (even now). Forming the role of a practitioner to become more than a function, and turning it into being a respected person, can often create this type of space.

About the Authors

Jerome Sewell

Jerome Sewell is an executive film producer, project manager, and managing director of two companies: one which assists young people from gang-hit communities called Unique Talent CIC where he heads their media and film department and their sustainable transport division Rollsafe, focused on the use of electric transport; he also runs a second company named Therapeutic Productions which provides mental health services through the creative arts. Over the last five years he has managed over 20 social projects, raised over £500,000 for community organizations, has been featured on the national news on three occasions for his social work, and has delivered services to over 400 service users through his companies. He also works for the Royal College of Psychiatrists as a service user representative, and has worked for the Recovery College (forensic campus) and Bethlem Royal Hospital, London, as an expert by experience, delivering presentations to over 300 mental health professionals, creating training material for NHS practitioners, and delivering psycho-educational courses to mental health patients.

Jerome is also an award-winning screenwriter, having won awards from the Koestler Awards and a leadership award from the Shackleton Foundation. As a writer he has published eight articles in a range of magazines including *Asylum* magazine, *OTNews* (the official magazine for the Royal College of Occupational Therapists), and the international title *TKD Times*. His work has also been taken on for book publication.

Lastly, in addition to the above, Jerome is someone with a lifelong interest and passion for East Asian traditional arts, philosophies, and practices. After starting his training in martial arts at the age of 7, he has gone on to write a number of articles on martial philosophy which encompassed the insights of some of the highest-ranked martial artists across seven different disciplines in the UK, with some being Olympic athletes such as Feyi Pearce, world champions such as Gavin McKenzie, and Buddhist monks such as Professor Kemmyo Taira Sato. This work earned him an honorary black belt awarded by Grandmaster Den Butler in Wiltshire for dedication to the study of martial philosophy and tradition, and these articles have also been featured in international publications such as the *TKD Times*. Later in life he would become a practitioner of internal styles of kung fu, particularly southern mantis, and has qualifications in Chinese medical practice whilst having practiced mindful meditation for over five years under Ron Maddox, former secretary of the Buddhist Society, and the mental health charity Mind.

Jason Harris

Jason Harris is a published poet and frontline peer support worker who provides one-on-one client-based support to those with psychiatric conditions through Norfolk and Suffolk Recovery College and the Social Recovery Team. Over the last five years he has provided support to over 100 service users and mental health workers. Jason also chairs the Hearing Voices Network, a support group for those experiencing hallucinations. As a worker for the Social Recovery Team, he organizes and supports a number of groups for those facing severe mental health conditions.

Mase Okor

Mase Okor is a Black-British performer and poet of Nigerian origin and was born in 1999, in South-East London where he still lives and works. He studied Drama and English Literature at the University of Greenwich. He has taken part in storytelling workshops to hone his craft and acting skills. He worked as an assistant director for a short film titled *Brother's Keeper*, which explores black single-parent households, brotherhood, and family.

Mase's work focuses primarily on gender and race, specifically masculinity and black identity. He explores these themes through the mediums of music, dance, and poetry to engage with his audience on an intellectual and intimate level. His inspirations draw heavily from posthumous and contemporary black artists and creators such as: James Baldwin; Chinua Achebe, a Nigerian Nobel Prize-winning novelist; Tristan Fynn-Aiduenu, a British-Ghanaian theatre-maker who co-directed *For Black Boys Who Have Considered Suicide When the Hue Gets Too Heavy* (2021); and Caleb Femi, a British-Nigerian poet who wrote the critically acclaimed poem collection *Poor* (2020).

Mase's music inspirations range from Nigerian multi-instrumentalist and Afrobeat pioneer Fela Kuti to Compton-born rapper and Pulitzer Prize-winner Kendrick Lamar. In using music to perform, Mase blends these genres with the consciousness of race, identity, and masculinity to further educate his audience.

Further Reading

Simpson, Sharon, Stewart Mercer, Robert Simpson, Maggie Lawrence, and Sally Wyke, "Mindfulness-Based Interventions for Young Offenders: A Scoping Review," *Mindfulness*, 2018.

Williams, Mark, and Danny Penman, *Mindfulness: Finding Peace in a Frantic World*, Piatkus, 2011.

References

Bentham, Jeremy, *An Introduction to the Principles of Morals and Legislation*, 1789.

Book of Ezekiel, King James Bible.

Chand, Suma P., Daniel P. Kuckel, and Martin R. Huecker, *Cognitive Behavior Therapy*, 2023.

Fogg, Ally, *Let's Be Rational about Gangs*, 2008.

Health Foundation, *Improving Health Outcomes of Young People by Developing Soft Skills*, 2017.

Holy Quran, chapter 7, verse 11.

Locke, John, *Two Treatises of Government*, 1689.

Matt, Kray, Tim Pritchard, and Wayne Hutchinson, *Once Upon a Time in Brixton*, 2021.

Office for National Statistics, *The Links between Young People Being Imprisoned, Pupil Background and School Quality*, 2023.

Price, Richard, *Principal Questions in Morals*, 1758, 3rd ed. revised 1787.

Sato, Kemmyo Taira, *D.T. Suzuki and the Question of War*, 2008.

Sewell, Jerome, "The Art of Occupation: Wielding the Mind," *OTNews*, 2019.

Sewell, Jerome, *Do You Have What It Takes?* Austin Macauley, 2024.

EASTERN RELIGION & PHILOSOPHY

We publish books on Eastern religions and philosophies. Books that aim to inform and explore the various traditions that began in the East and have migrated West.

If you have enjoyed this book, why not tell other readers by posting a review on your preferred book site.

Recent Bestsellers from MANTRA BOOKS Are:

The Way Things Are

A Living Approach to Buddhism

Lama Ole Nydahl

An introduction to the teachings of the Buddha, and how to make use of these teachings in everyday life.

Paperback: 978-1-84694-042-2 ebook: 978-1-78099-845-9

Back to the Truth

5000 Years of Advaita

Dennis Waite

A demystifying guide to Advaita for both those new to, and those familiar with this ancient, non-dualist philosophy from India.

Paperback: 978-1-90504-761-1 ebook: 978-184694-624-0

Shinto: A celebration of Life

Aidan Rankin

Introducing a gentle but powerful spiritual pathway reconnecting humanity with Great Nature and arming all aspects of life.

Paperback: 978-1-84694-438-3 ebook: 978-1-84694-738-4

In the Light of Meditation

Mike George

A comprehensive introduction to the practice of meditation and the spiritual principles behind it. A 10 lesson meditation programme with CD and internet support.

Paperback: 978-1-90381-661-5

The 7 Levels of Wisdom

Mónica Esgueva

A straightforward and compelling approach on how to reach the highest levels of consciousness, wisdom, and inner peace.

Paperback: 978-1-80341-470-6 ebook: 978-1-80341-471-3

Compassion Based Living Course

Heather Regan-Addis and Choden

A practical guide to living a compassionate life.

Paperback: 978-1-80341-676-2 ebook: 978-1-80341-709-7

The Sacred Gathas of Zarathushtra & the Old Avestan Canon

Pablo Vazquez

The ancient and mystical poetry of Zarathushtra and the first Zoroastrians: Now accessible to the public in a modern translation.

Paperback: 978-1-78535-961-3 ebook: 978-1-78535-962-0

Radiant Bliss

Sue Bushell

Embrace Your Journey: Unfolding Peace, Power, and Purpose Through Yoga

Paperback: 978-1-80341-818-6 ebook: 978-1-80341-822-3

Ordinary Women, Extraordinary Wisdom
Rita Marie Robinson
The Feminine Face of Awakening
A collection of intimate conversations with female spiritual teachers who live like ordinary women, but are engaged with their true natures.
Paperback: 978-1-84694-068-2 ebook: 978-1-78099-908-1

The Riddle of Alchemy
Paul Kiritsis
What is alchemy, exactly? Is there any empirical truth to ancient speculative pursuits toward metallic transmutation? How does alchemy intersect with Western mind sciences and science in general?
Paperback: 978-1-80341-637-3 ebook: 978-1-80341-688-5

Readers of ebooks can buy or view any of these bestsellers by clicking on the live link in the title. Most titles are published in paperback and as an ebook. Paperbacks are available in traditional bookshops. Both print and ebook formats are available online.

Find more titles and sign up to our readers' newsletter at www.collectiveinkbooks.com/mind-body-spirit. Follow us on Facebook at facebook.com/OBooks and Twitter at twitter.com/obooks